EVERYDAY
TWITTER
MADE EASY

This edition first published 2014 by
FLAME TREE PUBLISHING
Crabtree Hall, Crabtree Lane
Fulham, London SW6 6TY
United Kingdom

www.flametreepublishing.com

14 16 18 17 15
1 3 5 7 9 10 8 6 4 2

© 2014 Flame Tree Publishing

ISBN 978-1-78361-234-5

A CIP record for this book is available from the British Library upon request.

Printed in China

All non-screenshot pictures are courtesy of Shutterstock and © the following photographers: Aaron Amat: 109; Andresr: 6, 116; antb: 142; baranq: 196; Peter Bernik: 18, 190, 232; Mircea Bezergheanu: 78; bikeriderlondon: 35; Gil C: 252; dolphfyn: 123; Dean Drobot: 230; everything possible: 7, 182; Juergen Faelchle: 218; Goodluz: 125, 139; Hasloo Group Production Studio: 12; Brian A. Jackson: 90; Stuart Jenner: 42; Ryan Jorgensen-Jorgo: 111; Jan Krcmar: 189; lculig: 3; Ldprod: 76, 242; lightwavemedia: 241; Eugenio Marongiu: 6, 81, 148; Kostenko Maxim: 115; michaeljung: 26, 223; Monkey Business Images: 163, 224; Brett Nattrass: 166; Naypong: 251; nenetus: 168; NicoElNino: 164; nopporn: 7, 216; Phase4Studios: 131; photastic: 234; PiXXart: 5, 46; Fabiana Ponzi: 37; Andrey_Popov: 101, 228; Pressmaster: 194; Ivelin Radkov: 5, 82; Sergey Nivens: 4, 14; Annette Shaff: 114; StockLite: 99; Syda Productions: 95; Twin Design: 1, 162, 226; Tyler Olson: 172, 174, 246; Vitchanan Photography: 136; wavebreakmedia: 63; Elena Yakusheva: 70; zeljkodan: 71

EVERYDAY
TWITTER
MADE EASY

RICHARD N. WILLIAMS

FLAME TREE
PUBLISHING

CONTENTS

Since it was first established in 2006, Twitter has become something of a phenomenon. Easy to sign up to, simple to use, Twitter is now one of the most popular social networking sites on the planet, with over 650 million users. This chapter will give you the lowdown on when it all started, how it works, what a hashtag is, why people use it and, more importantly, where it will take you.

TWITTER BASICS 46

Now that you have decided to enter the Twittersphere, you need to know what to do there. This chapter will help you set up your Twitter persona (your account, profile and handle), understand the Twitter interface and get to grips with Twitter jargon. It will show you the different ways to access Twitter from your computer or handheld device and, once you've found them, how to group your followers into lists.

THE TWEET 82

Lots to say, but only 140 characters in which to say it? This word limit is one of Twitter's most appealing aspects, but also one of its greatest challenges. In this chapter, as well as learning how to tweet and what to tweet about, you will find out some of the secrets behind effective tweeting, including setting the right tone, editing your tweet and when to tweet. It also explains the mechanics behind more of Twitter's celebrated features: retweets, replies and mentions.

Twitter is all about what people are saying, so whether you use Twitter for socializing or as a way of promoting your business, it is essential to find like-minded users to receive tweets from and send tweets to. This chapter is all about you and your followers: how to discover them, how to contact them and how many you are allowed to follow. It will also show you how to avoid following potentially harmful accounts, and what to do if you want to unfollow someone.

This chapter will show you how you can make the most of Twitter, whether you want to tweet for business or pleasure, from your computer, smartphone or tablet. Discover how you can use Twitter as a search engine, hold a Q&A session, add a link to a website, promote a tweet for advertising purposes and integrate your Twitter feed with Facebook. Should you encounter negative behaviour, advice on how to deal with the perpetrator is given.

TWITTER FOR BUSINESS

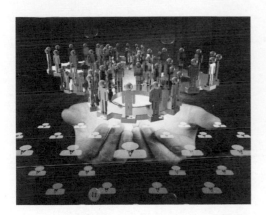

Whether your organization employs one or 1,000, you want the world to know about what you do, and Twitter is a platform that can help you reach millions of potential customers. But you have to get it right, as it's easy for your carefully crafted tweets to get buried. This chapter will show you how Twitter can work for your business, by engaging with followers and building your brand, and how to target your tweets and stand out from the crowd.

ADVANCED TWITTER

Once you become familiar with Twitter, you will want to know what more it can do for you. This chapter will help you take your usage to the next level, by learning about Twitter's privacy rules and regulations and the potential pitfalls of saying what you think (twibel), as well as how it can be used to promote a portfolio of work, to hold conferences and to give testimonials. You will see how to manage multiple accounts by using Twitter clients, and how to troubleshoot when things go wrong.

INTRODUCTION

Twitter is among the fastest-growing and most influential social networking service around. If you want to make the most of it, either for business or pleasure, *Everyday Twitter Made Easy* will show you how.

TWITTER

There are not many people who have not heard of Twitter. Apart from revolutionizing the way we communicate, this social media platform has become one of the fastest ways of getting news and information. Often, stories break on Twitter long before traditional news outlets can report them, and Twitter is also in the news itself, creating controversy and letting the world know what was happening in revolutions such as the Arab Spring.

Universal Access

Twitter offers almost anybody a platform to share their views and opinions with the rest of the world. Not only that, but people now have unrivalled access to those in the news. You can follow your favourite celebrity, the president of the United States or even the Pope. Furthermore, you can send these people messages and they may even message you back.

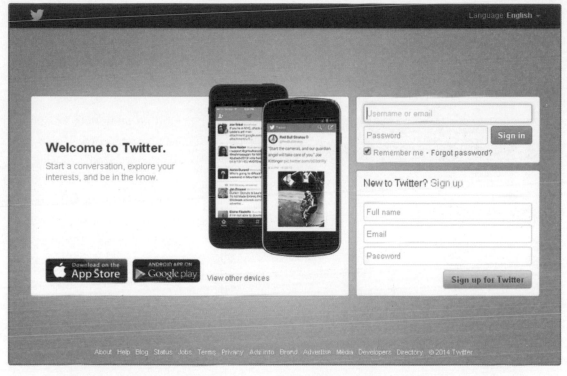

Above: Join Twitter to get the latest news, follow your favourite celebrity and share your views with the rest of the world.

TWITTER MADE EASY

Everybody seems to be on Twitter, these days. If you feel like you are missing out and want to join in this social media revolution, but are unsure how, this book is for you. We will provide you with all the information you need to join the Twittersphere, and take part in one of the most exciting and influential social media platforms around. Inside this book, you will learn how to do the following:

Hot Tip

Throughout this book, we have inserted a number of Hot Tips. These are designed to help you find some simple yet effective methods to get the most out of Twitter.

○ **Open an account**: We will tell you what you need to register for Twitter and show you how to sign up.

○ **Messaging**: We will explain the tweet and show you how to send and receive them.

○ **Find an audience**: You will learn how to follow people and build up your own following.

○ **Twitter feed**: We will also take you through your Twitter interface, where you can see the messages that the people you are following have sent.

○ **Interacting**: We will also explain how to reply to tweets, send direct messages, and explain what retweets and mentions are.

Above: The Tweet box interface is where you can compose a tweet and check your followers and following count.

TWEETING

The tweet is what makes Twitter unique. With only 140 characters, it can be difficult to learn how to fit in what you want to say. However, we will give you hints and tips to help you tweet successfully, and show you how to insert links and images into your tweets to make them more engaging.

Retweets, Replies, Mentions and Direct Messages

Twitter is all about social interaction; we will not only show you how to send and receive tweets, but also how to reply to what people have said, mention other users in tweets and share comments by retweeting them. You will also discover how to send direct messages on Twitter, thus enabling you to speak privately to people.

FOLLOWING AND FOLLOWERS

There is little point in tweeting if nobody is listening to what you say. Twitter works by a system of following and followers. The latter are those people who receive your messages, while you receive tweets from people you are following. Building up your followers on Twitter can be difficult, but we will show you how to attract an audience and widen your reach so that as many people as possible see your tweets.

Above: Twitter interactions include mentioning other users in your tweets, retweeting and sending direct messages.

TWITTER FOR BUSINESS

Twitter is not just great for socializing; it is also a brilliant tool for promotion and raising brand awareness. If you run a business or have something you would like to promote, we will show how you can use Twitter to reach millions of potential new customers, raise the profile of your business and see what other people are saying about you.

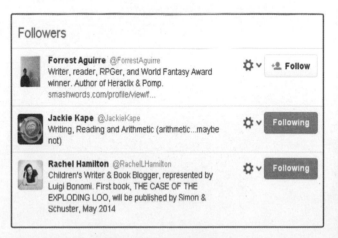

Above: Followers are the people who receive your messages.

USING THIS BOOK

We have tried to make this book as useful as possible for those new to Twitter as well as those already using it. We have organized the chapters to make it easy for you to find the information you need and, therefore, do not feel like you have to read every page of this book in order; use it as a reference to help you along the way.

Hot Tip

Twitter is an American platform and some of its features use American spellings. In order to avoid confusion, we have kept these spellings when mentioning specific features, such as Favorites, but use British spellings elsewhere.

Twitter Tips

Inside, you will find a whole raft of hints, tips and tricks to help you make better use of Twitter and maximize its potential. You will learn how to use apps on your phone, find people to follow and make targeted searches.

Step-by-step

Throughout this book, we have included step-by-step guides to steer you through some of the more technical aspects of Twitter, such as setting up your profile page, uploading images or organizing your followers

Above: Download the Twitter app on your mobile phone to keep up to date with new tweets wherever you go.

Twitter Terminology

Twitter is full of its own jargon and terminology. However, we have tried to explain some of the more common terms and acronyms, as well as providing you with instructions and information using the simplest possible terms.

Advanced Twitter

If you are already familiar with Twitter, but want to take your usage to the next stage, we will help you to boost your following and make your profile more appealing, as well as showing you how to use Twitter clients to manage multiple accounts and organize your followers.

TWITTER CLIENTS

As mentioned above, Twitter clients are extremely useful, for a variety of reasons (as you will discover), as are Twitter-related web services, of which there are many. We have included a list of some of the best (in our opinion) at the end of the book, but please note that access to them may be restricted and the cost of purchasing or downloading them is subject to change.

Tweet Tweet
Tweet
Tweet
Tweet
Tweet tweet
tweet
Tweet Tweet
Tweet
tweet
Tweet tweet
Tweet tweet
Tweet

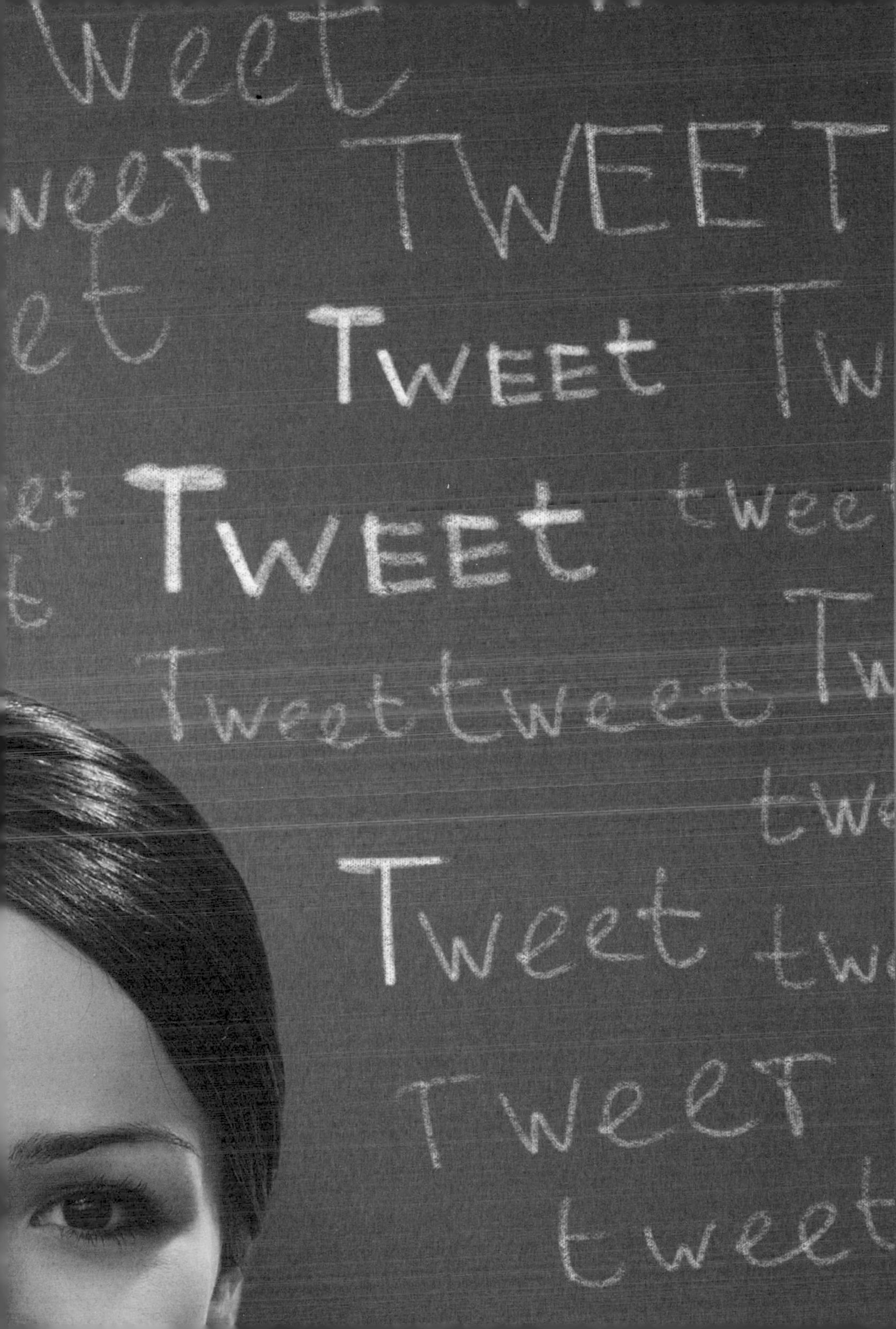

WHY TWEET?

BACKGROUND

Most people have heard of Twitter; the social networking site has become a phenomenon. Not only is Twitter a way for people to communicate, socialize and access news and information, but it also often makes the news itself.

MICROBLOGGING

Twitter is a microblogging site. Microblogging is similar to other forms of blogging, where people can write what they like, be it their views, opinions or just what is happening around them. The only difference is in the size of each post.

The Tweet

The posts written by Twitter users are known as 'tweets'. Those with a Twitter account can both read and write tweets, but anybody can access Twitter and read what people are writing about. tweets are limited in size to 140 characters. This has its roots in Twitter's history, as the platform was designed for use with SMS (Short Message Service) text messages. However, this has made Twitter an ideal social network for the modern world, where people increasingly want short bursts of information rather than long-winded blog posts and news stories.

Above: Twitter posts are called tweets and are limited in size to 140 characters.

SOCIAL NETWORK

Twitter falls under the category of a social network. In other words, it is an online platform where people can find and communicate with friends, make connections and meet like-minded individuals. As a social network, Twitter has some unique features that make it a little different to other social network platforms such as Facebook.

Followers and Following

Users of Twitter 'follow' other users. This process of following enables people to find like-minded individuals or sources of information in which they may be interested. Essentially, following somebody means that you are subscribing to that person's Twitter feed. So whenever people post a tweet, this is sent to all those who are following them, who can then reply and comment. By default, tweets are publicly available, which means that anybody can search and read the posts, but users can restrict tweets to just their followers if they so wish.

Ease of Use

One thing that makes Twitter so appealing to people is its simplicity. Sending and receiving tweets is incredibly straightforward, meaning that anybody can sign up and begin tweeting almost immediately. Twitter is also widely accessible, as even those without an account can see tweets and read what people are saying.

Hot Tip

Twitter has a system called 'retweets', where people can forward posts to all their followers, thus helping to broaden the reach of interesting tweets beyond a user's own followers.

Above: Following someone means subscribing to that person's Twitter feed. To share an interesting tweet, retweet it.

Versatile

Since Twitter is so simple and easy to use, it is incredibly versatile. People can send tweets on a computer, laptop, tablet and phone. This means that people can tweet and keep abreast of what people are saying – wherever they are.

Immediacy

This versatility and ease of use also make Twitter very immediate. The fact that tweets are available to read as soon as somebody posts them has made Twitter a powerful media platform. When a news story breaks, Twitter users often report it long before TV networks and other media outlets have a chance to broadcast it. This has turned Twitter into an incredibly useful tool for finding news and up-to-date information.

TWITTER HISTORY

Twitter is a relatively new social network. It all began in 2006, when podcasting company Odeo created a short message service for its staff to be able to communicate with each other. However, the company soon realized that they had a potentially powerful social networking tool, and Twitter was launched to the world in July 2006. In April 2007, Twitter became its own company and by the end of 2013, it was estimated to be worth more than $32.76 billion (£19.7 billion).

Hot Tip

Odeo's Jack Dorsey published the world's first tweet at 12:50 p.m. (Pacific Standard Time) on 21 March 2006. It read: 'just setting up my twttr', which was the working name for the project that was to become Twitter.

Growth

The growth of Twitter has been incredible: from just 20,000 users in 2007 to over half a billion people regularly using it by the end of 2013. In addition, twitter.com receives nearly 200 million unique page views a year, making it the tenth most popular website on the planet, while a billion tweets are sent every five days.

Above: Twitter's founder Jack Dorsey published the first tweet on 21 March 2006.

Twitter Today

Twitter has moved on from being a simple social messaging service. Nowadays, Twitter apps enable anybody with a smartphone to send and receive tweets, while features such as photo sharing and expanded tweets have added more functionality. Everybody – from the US president to the Pope, and including countless celebrities – has Twitter accounts, and people have even tweeted from outer space and from the ocean floor. Twitter was also thought to have been a crucial component that enabled the Arab Spring uprisings in early 2011.

TWITTER MILESTONES

- **March 2006**: First tweet sent by Twitter founder Jack Dorsey.

- **July 2006**: Twitter launched to the public.

- **April 2009**: Actor Ashton Kutcher becomes the first person to accumulate one million followers.

- **January 2010**: Astronaut Timothy Creamer sends a tweet from space, saying: 'Hello Twitterverse!'

Above: Barack Obama's famous 'four more years' tweet was retweeted by over 500,000 people.

- **January 2011**: Twitter and Facebook play a key role in the 'Arab Spring' uprisings.

- **November 2012**: After his successful re-election, President Barack Obama tweeted: 'Four more years', which was retweeted by over 500,000 people.

- **September 2013**: Twitter announces it will sell shares in the company on the US stock exchange.

ADVANTAGES

Twitter users are part of one of the world's leading online communities, and this popularity has a lot to do with the many advantages that Twitter offers over other social networks and web services.

COMMUNITY

Being on Twitter is like being part of an exclusive club. Yet, anybody can join it, follow anybody they like and say whatever is on their mind. The Twitter community is by and large a friendly one, and many people find that they can build up a large network of followers and Twitter friends from all over the world.

Above: Twitter's global community, known as the 'Twitterverse', allows users access to people from all over the world.

Twitterverse

Twitter is truly global, with users in almost every country on the planet. This global community is known as the 'Twitterverse' or 'Twittersphere'. Unlike other social networking platforms, such as Facebook, which are popular with teenagers and young people, Twitter users tend to fall into older demographics, with nearly 90 per cent of the Twittersphere being over 18. Slightly more women than men are on Twitter, too: 53 per cent compared to 47 per cent.

FOLLOWING AND FOLLOWERS

The system of following and being followed is unique to Twitter and, unlike other social networks, you do not need to be accepted by the person you want to follow. This offers users access to all sorts of people and organizations.

Here are the sorts of accounts that people follow on Twitter.

- ○ **Organizations**: Most businesses and large organizations now have a Twitter presence, enabling them to communicate to customers directly.

- ○ **Friends**: Twitter lets you keep abreast of what your friends are up to, as well as message them directly.

- ○ **Celebrities**: Musicians, authors and actors now have Twitter accounts, offering fans unrivalled access to their lives.

Hot Tip

If you do not want just anybody following you, you can set your Twitter account to private; this allows you to approve people before they can follow you.

- ○ **News outlets**: Most large news organizations post updates on Twitter.

- ○ **Politicians**: From the US President to the British Prime Minister, politicians regularly use Twitter to communicate with the electorate.

Left: Twitter allows users to connect with the accounts of organizations, friends, celebrities, news outlets and politicians.

SIMPLICITY

Perhaps the main reason Twitter is so popular is its simplicity. Twitter is streamlined and straightforward, which means that it is easy to set up an account, follow and begin tweeting.

Easy to Join

Anybody with an email address can join Twitter; indeed, it takes just a couple of minutes to sign up. Even if you do not wish to register, you can still access the Twitter interface at twitter.com/search-home to read tweets, search for celebrities and see what is trending (although unregistered users cannot follow or send tweets).

Easy to Use

Sending tweets, following, retweeting and searching for information is incredibly easy on Twitter. The simple user interface needs little explanation and new users can begin tweeting from the moment they sign up.

Access

As a communication tool, Twitter offers incredible freedom. No other social media platform allows people to communicate directly with their favourite pop star, actor or celebrity. Users can post questions directly to people in the public eye, strike up conversations and retweet their comments.

Above: Twitter is easy to join, easy to use and it is easy to access your favourite pop star; Lady Gaga has over 41 million Twitter followers.

PROMOTION

Twitter has become an invaluable tool for promotion, as it enables all sorts of people to advertise their products and services. Businesses, organizations, bloggers, musicians, authors and even charities can reach thousands – or even millions – of people on Twitter. Twitter campaigns are now a common part of most marketing strategies, as few other promotional activities offer such reach. Twitter also offers advertising known as promoted tweets, which are displayed at the top of people's Twitter feeds.

SHARING

Twitter is an easy way to swap all sorts of media, including the following:

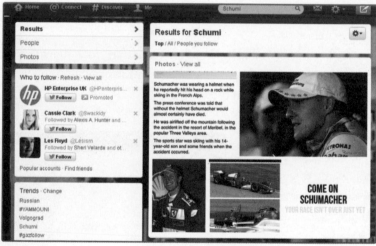

- **Links**: Twitter enables you to send links to blogs and websites.

- **Photos**: Users can attach photos to their tweets on twitter.com or by using a third-party service like TwitPic.

Above: Pictures, videos and links to blogs and websites are tweeted to promote companies' products and services.

- **Videos**: Users can send links to media-sharing websites such as YouTube or Vimeo.

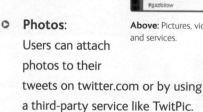

Hot Tip

Twitter has an app service called Vine, which allows smartphone users to upload short (six-second) video clips and attach them to their posts.

MESSAGING

You can use Twitter as a simple messaging service and send somebody two types of messages:

- **Public**: The message that you send to somebody will be publicly visible.

- **Private**: Direct messages (DMs) allow you to send private messages to individual followers that only that person can see.

NEWS

Twitter is one of the most effective ways of keeping up to date with what is happening. News often breaks on Twitter long before it does in mainstream media outlets. In addition, you can use hashtag searches (*see* pages 103–105) to find out the latest on specific subjects. Most news organizations now use Twitter to post headlines and breaking stories.

Trending Topics

Using the hashtag system, Twitter is able to list all the popular topics at any given time. These are known as trending topics and mean that users can see which news stories are breaking or what the rest of the world is talking about.

Right: Direct messages (DMs) allow you to send private messages to individual followers that only that person can see.

Hot Tip

Twitter is the perfect tool for arranging meetings with lots of people, as you can set a time and place between you all, without one person having to keep messaging people individually.

Direct messages › **New**	✕

140   Send message

Information

If you need information on something or want to know the answer to a question, asking the Twittersphere is one of the quickest ways to get a response. And even if your friends and followers cannot help, quite often it is not long before your message is retweeted to somebody who can give you the answer.

AUTOMATION

Third-party services such as HootSuite enable users to schedule and post automated messages. This sort of automation enables people to use Twitter as a promotional tool and keep an active presence without having to log on all the time.

Above: Email notification from Twitter allows you to stay connected with your account even when you're offline.

Notifications

Twitter also provides automated notifications so that you can keep abreast of when you have a direct message, are mentioned in a tweet or have a new follower. This enables you to monitor your Twitter account without actually having to log on.

DISADVANTAGES

No social network is perfect, and Twitter does have its problems, so it is perhaps wise to understand the disadvantages before you decide whether tweeting is for you.

SIZE

With its millions of users, and millions of tweets being sent every day, Twitter is huge. This sheer number of people tweeting, retweeting and following means that, as a newcomer to Twitter, getting your posts read and acquiring followers can be a challenge.

Voice in the Crowd

For anybody new to Twitter, there is no way of knowing whether your tweets are actually being read. In fact, the only statistics that Twitter provides you with to help you to ascertain the success of your messages are how many people retweeted them or marked them as favourite tweets (see pages 114 and 150).

Buried Tweets

Many Twitter users have hundreds, even thousands, of followers so it is very

Right: New tweets always appear at the top of the Twitter feed, but disappear quickly due to the large number of new tweets appearing frequently.

Gautam Trivedi @Gotham3   39s
There is an undo mechanism for people you hate. I guess it's called murder.
Expand   ← Reply ⇄ Retweet ★ Favorite ••• More

Faydra Deon @faydra_deon   43s
#Kindle Freebie: Intents & Purposes by Simon Temprell: vew.im/o30f #ebblitz
🗋 View summary   ← Reply ⇄ Retweet ★ Favorite ••• More

Faydra Deon @faydra_deon   46s
You could be making money just by getting people to visit the Independent Author Index: v1s.it/JvVBOM #iaindex
Expand   ← Reply ⇄ Retweet ★ Favorite ••• More

Mohana Rajakumar @moha_doha   1m
Canned Goods Make Me Happy & I'm Not Alone Sponsored #CansGetYouCooking goo.gl/zlHJyw via @mamasmoney

Hot Tip

In order to write concisely, learn Twitter Speak, i.e. the language of Twitter, which includes a host of abbreviations that can make writing what you want to say in 140 characters much easier.

easy for tweets to become quickly buried. New tweets always appear at the top of a Twitter feed, and it does not take long before they disappear from view.

TWITTER LIMITATIONS

There are limits to what Twitter can do, and many of its features can be quite restrictive and even frustrating. However, Twitter changes its functionality quite frequently.

140 Characters

One of Twitter's most appealing aspects, the 140-character limit is also one of its most limiting factors. For newcomers especially, getting down what they want to say in such a small space can be a real challenge.

Above: New programs like Vine allow users to embed videos and images into their tweets, extending the 140-character limit.

Embedded Media

While Twitter now allows embedded images in tweets, it's limited when it comes to video posting. External sites such as YouTube allow you to embed videos into a tweet, but you cannot upload them; however, this may change in the future, especially with new services like Twitter Vine.

Messaging

Although you can send direct messages (DMs) on Twitter and speak privately to your followers – just like sending an email or text – unlike other DM systems adopted by social networks such as Facebook, you cannot send a private message to more than one person at a time. If you wish to send a direct message to more than one follower, you have to send it individually. This can be frustrating, especially if you need to send a DM to a hundred or so people.

Following

While you can pretty much choose who you follow on Twitter (other than people with protected accounts; see pages 89 and 122), you are limited to a set number of followers. Each Twitter user can follow only 2,000 people before restrictions set in. You can follow more people after this but it depends on the number of people who are following you. In addition,

Above: Each user can only follow 2,000 people before restrictions set in. For follower-to-following ratio information, visit the Twitter support page.

Twitter does not publish this follower-to-following ratio, so some users suddenly find that they are unable to follow any more people, unless they start unfollowing accounts.

SPAM

Since it is so easy to set up an account and automate tweets, Twitter is an easy place for spammers to operate. While Twitter does a lot to detect and eliminate spam and spambots (an automated computer program that sends spam), they still exist. Spammers also keep coming up with clever ways to get you to click on links to external websites, such as suggesting that there is an embarrassing photograph of you.

Hot Tip

Never log on to your Twitter account using a link sent to you by email. Always use the official Twitter address, twitter.com.

SECURITY ISSUES

Worse than the spammers on Twitter are the scammers, who often use phishing tactics to extract your login details. These scammers often set up a fake Twitter homepage and send you an email claiming that you have a new direct message or follower in order to obtain your account details when you visit their site.

Hacked Accounts

If you have fallen victim to a fake Twitter webpage and handed over your details, you may find that your Twitter account ends up being hacked. Usually, this involves the

Left: To avoid spam, always login to your Twitter account using the official Twitter address: twitter.com.

scammers pretending to be you and sending tweets to your followers, often asking them to click on a link. However, Twitter is normally quick to act when your account has been hacked and will reset your password for you (*see* pages 244–245).

PRIVACY

As with other social networks, Twitter shares the information that you give with third parties, namely advertisers. Many people feel concerned about this data sharing. In addition, as anybody on Twitter can see your personal profile and read your tweets, it is easy for people with malicious intent to use your details for fraud, identity theft and other criminal activities, which is why you need to be careful with the information you supply.

Hot Tip

If you find yourself the victim of a troll, block the user from following your feed and report the matter to Twitter.

Trolls

As Twitter allows anyone with an email address to set up an account, it is easy to remain anonymous. However, this has its problems, as some users use the platform to send offensive and malicious tweets – a practice known as trolling.

Above: Sending offensive and malicious tweets to others is known as trolling; in 2013, the BBC broadcast a news story about Twitter trolling being on the rise.

TWITTER SPEAK

As users need to condense their messages into 140 characters, a lot of abbreviations and jargon have arisen on Twitter. At first, Twitter Speak can be confusing and takes some deciphering. For a breakdown of some of the most common Twitter terminology, see chapter two.

LEGAL ISSUES

Twitter's emergence has brought with it a number of controversies. Most of these have arisen because of legal issues with what people have tweeted. Since Twitter is so easy to use and anybody can tweet what they like, it is very easy for people to send libellous messages or

Above: Twitter Speak, a set of abbreviations and jargon used on Twitter, is used to condense messages into 140 characters.

discuss subjects that may have other legal consequences, such as ongoing court cases. For more information governing legal issues on Twitter, *see* pages 226–234.

TIME

There is no doubt that Twitter can be addictive and steal a lot of your free time. Some people become too immersed in the Twittersphere, resulting in a lot of lost time. It is also easy to become obsessed with obtaining followers and getting retweets, so if your work or home life starts to suffer because of your incessant tweeting, try to take a break – or at least reduce the time you spend on Twitter.

Outages

Twitter is also a victim of its own success. Since so many people are opening accounts every day and joining the Twitterverse, the servers can often get overloaded, thus resulting in outages. This can be frustrating if you are in the middle of a conversation or have a direct message you cannot access because you cannot log in.

TWITTER MANAGEMENT

When you have built up a large following and are following lots of people, it can be extremely difficult to manage all of them, especially since Twitter does not let you create groups. However, you can create lists (*see* pages 77–81) and some third-party apps can help you to manage your account.

3,518	16,014	16,003
TWEETS	FOLLOWING	FOLLOWERS

Tweets

The Site: Art Online @fantasysite
Hot Product! Nike + Sport Watch GPS Powered by Tom Tom (WHITE) + 1 Sensor bit.ly/1h8zl96
View details   ← Reply ⟲ Retweet ★ Favorite

Above: Lists and some third-party apps can help you manage your account if you have a huge following and are following many users.

PSYCHOLOGY BEHIND TWITTER

Twitter's dramatic rise in popularity has raised a lot of interest from psychologists, who want to know what drives people to share almost every aspect of their daily lives with others.

THE TWITTER OBSESSION

Twitter's simplicity, its flexibility (it's now possible to tweet on smartphones) and its easy-to-use nature have resulted in some people sending hundreds of tweets every day. These sorts of Twitter users write about almost everything that happens in their day-to-day lives, from what they have had for breakfast to when they are feeling tired. The reasons people feel the need to share so much of their lives with their followers, many of whom are complete strangers, have been the subject of much research.

119	484	485
TWEETS	FOLLOWING	FOLLOWERS

Just getting out of bed ... yawn #sotired

#SoTired

COMMUNICATION

Fundamentally, Twitter is another communication platform. Although we have mobile phones, text messaging and numerous other social networks and means to communicate with one another, Twitter has filled a communication need: the ability to express our thoughts to large numbers of people in real time.

Left: Many users share information about their daily lives because they are able to express their thoughts to large numbers of people in real time.

Community

Twitter has become a global community. It has allowed people to have real-time conversations with multiple individuals across the globe, which is something that other social networks and messaging services cannot do as effectively. Psychologists suggest that people are inherently gregarious social beings who are used to living in communities, and Twitter provides a way to be part of a large social group. Furthermore, not being on Twitter can make people feel like they are missing out – a bit like being the only person not invited to the party.

> **Hot Tip**
>
> Twitter is not just a great place to meet new people, but is also a useful tool for keeping in touch with existing friends, colleagues and associates.

Friendship

Many people also join Twitter to build up friendships. Psychologists suggest that society and community have changed over the last few decades, and social networks such as Twitter are filling the void left by traditional meeting places. Twitter helps people to find like-minded individuals and to share opinions with those who share similar views, as well as to form connections with those interested in the same subjects and passions.

SELF-EXPRESSION

Another reason Twitter is so popular is the need that people have to express themselves. Although not everybody is an artist, author or musician, psychologists suggest that we all have a need to express our thoughts, opinions and views. Conversation is important for people, and, in a society where people are becoming ever more detached and distant from one another, Twitter offers the closest thing to real conversation available in the virtual world. It is also completely egalitarian, as anybody can join Twitter and say what is on their mind.

Freedom

Twitter also offers people a freedom hitherto not experienced, as they can now have closer access to celebrities, actors, musicians and politicians than ever before. Almost anyone can send a message to their favourite pop star or movie star – something that was difficult to do before Twitter came along.

Twitter Persona

People can create a new persona on Twitter, as most of their followers won't know who they are. This anonymity can encourage some people to say things and express themselves in a way that may be very different from their behaviour in the real world.

Above: People join Twitter because it gives them freedom and anonymity to express themselves in a new way.

TWITTER ADDICTION

Without doubt, some people have become addicted to and obsessed with Twitter. This may be down to the way it functions, as many of its aspects – such as collecting followers, and getting retweets and mentions – create a need similar to that of other obsessive behaviours, such as collecting stamps or achieving a high score on a video game.

Need for Information

Finally, Twitter satisfies the human need for information. It is one of the best platforms for finding out what is going on in the world. Twitter is great for finding out news, hearing about new books, films and music, and learning what other people in the world are talking about. This helps to sate our thirst for knowledge, but it does have a downside, as, when we turn Twitter off, we can be left with the feeling that we might be missing out on something.

Hot Tip

Twitter is a great tool and social networking platform, but you should not let it rule your life. Avoid looking at your Twitter feed too often in order to prevent it from becoming an obsession.

WHY DO YOU WANT TO TWEET?

Is Twitter for you? Simply signing up without knowing what you want out of Twitter may result in you soon getting bored or frustrated. Knowing why you want to tweet is important if you want to get the most out of the platform.

YOUR TWITTER

People join Twitter for many different reasons, and knowing why you want to be part of the Twitterverse can help you to understand whether this platform is for you. It will also help you to reach your Twitter goals.

YOU WANT TO CONNECT WITH PEOPLE

Many people sign up to Twitter to meet new people. As more of our life moves to the internet, many of us find that meeting new people is increasingly difficult. Although you will probably never see face to face most of the people you connect with on Twitter, it is still a great place to socialize and chat.

Friends

As with other social networks, Twitter is a great place to chat with friends, colleagues and family members. No matter where people you know are in the world, joining Twitter makes it easy to keep in touch.

Left: Join Twitter to stay connected with friends, colleagues and family members around the world.

Corporate Connections

Many people in the business world find Twitter an invaluable tool. Its hashtags are more and more frequently being used to promote conferences and events, while many people in the corporate world use Twitter to connect with others in their industry.

Organizations and Causes

Twitter is the perfect way to follow and interact with organizations and charities about which you are passionate.

Hot Tip

If you intend to use Twitter for work, ensure that you do your research on the common hashtags used by your industry in order to help you find relevant people and tweets.

Above: Twitter is used as a tool in the business world. Many organizations, such as Greenpeace, use Twitter's hashtag to promote their conferences and events.

YOU WANT TO BE PART OF THE TWITTERVERSE

Another common reason for people to sign up to Twitter is because everybody else is on it. Many people are curious about what goes on in the Twitterverse and feel like they are missing out. However, those who join Twitter just out of curiosity soon abandon it. In order to get the most out of this platform, you really need to have a reason or goal for signing up.

Hot Tip

If you are thinking of signing up to Twitter to express your views and opinions or to share your expertise, consider starting a blog too. Tweeting is a great way to complement blog posts.

Trends · Change

Russian
#YAMMOUNI
Volgograd
Schumi
#paranoia
#gazfollow
#QnA
#AskMike
Xinjiang
Samsung to Launch 110-Inch Ultra HD

YOU WANT TO KNOW WHAT'S GOING ON

Nothing is better at keeping you abreast of what is going on than Twitter. News travels faster on Twitter than on TV, websites, blogs, radio and newspapers. Breaking stories often appear on Twitter before anywhere else, and journalists often tweet links to their stories and articles as soon as they are published online.

What's Hot

If you want to know what people are talking about, Twitter is the ideal platform to keep abreast of the latest fashions. Twitter is a great way to find out what music, films or TV shows are popular at the moment, and trending topics will give you an idea as to who or what is making the news at present.

YOU HAVE SOMETHING TO SAY

If you are somebody who likes debating current affairs, Twitter is the platform for you. You can speak to journalists, comment on news stories and discuss politics with your

Left: Twitter's trending topics are a great way to keep abreast of what is going on around the world.

followers. Twitter is a great platform for debating your opinions, and is also perfect if you have skills and knowledge that you want to share.

YOU WANT TO FOLLOW CELEBRITIES

If you are a fan of a particular band, pop star, actor or TV star, Twitter lets you get up close and personal. Not only can you follow your favourite celebrities and find out what they are doing and what projects they are involved in, but Twitter also allows you to message them. Whether your tweet is read may be another matter, but few other social network platforms allow you to get so close to celebrities.

Sports Fans

Another good reason to get involved with Twitter is if you are into sports. You can follow your favourite teams or players to hear the latest news, as well as chat to other fans. Since Twitter is also immediate, you can even comment and express your views during matches and games.

Above: Join Twitter to start your own Twitter blog, follow celebrities, or keep up with your favourite sports team.

YOU WANT TO PROMOTE SOMETHING

If you have a business you want to market, are an author with a book out, a band with a new album or have a brand you want to market, joining Twitter is a good idea. Twitter is fast becoming an essential marketing and promotional tool which will allow you to promote your goods and services and build up brand awareness. Tweeting regularly will let you connect to people and boost your visibility.

YOU HAVE TIME TO FILL

Finally, if you have a little time, Twitter is fun and a great way to while away those spare minutes each day, such as when waiting for a bus or an appointment. Twitter is not time wasted though; there is so much going on in the Twittersphere, which means that it is a fantastic place to learn new things, stay informed and meet new people. In addition, it can be a lot of fun building up followers and you will experience some satisfaction when the things you say are retweeted.

Left: Twitter is fast becoming an essential marketing and promotional tool, which will allow you to promote your goods and services, and build up brand awareness.

TWITTER USES

Just as there are a multitude of reasons to start tweeting, Twitter has plenty of uses. It isn't just a great platform to connect and communicate with people; it also has some distinct functions.

MICROBLOGGING PLATFORM

Essentially, Twitter is a microblogging platform and therefore shares the same uses as other types of online blogging platforms. Twitter gives you the ability to speak to the world, but it can do this more effectively than, say, a regular blog, as it comes with its own audience.

- **Opinions, news and views:** Whether you are a professional journalist or somebody with a need to know what is happening, Twitter is by far the best platform for keeping abreast of what is going on.

- **Sharing:** As with other blogs, Twitter is useful for sharing thoughts, opinions, pictures and links to other websites.

Above: Twitter gives the ability to speak to the world, making it an excellent platform to get news, share views and opinions and promote products.

- **Promotion:** If you have something to promote, Twitter is an invaluable tool.

- **Connecting with people:** Twitter is incredibly useful for finding people with similar interests or who work in the same industry as you.

UP-TO-THE-MINUTE INFORMATION

Tweeting is quick and immediate, which makes Twitter useful for finding the latest information on a range of topics.

Hot Tip

If you want to lose weight, use the hashtag #tweetwhatyoueat, which lets you make public what you eat. This is a great way to be more mindful of what you are consuming and can help you to lose weight.

- **News**: Stories can break on Twitter as soon as they happen.

- **Travel**: By following local news stations and traffic centres, you can get up-to-the-minute traffic reports.

- **Weather**: By following the Met Office or other weather organizations, you can keep up to date with the weather forecast.

Above: Since some stories break on Twitter as soon as they happen, it's a great way of getting travel and weather updates.

ADVICE

If you want a restaurant recommendation, need to know how to fix something or are looking for recipe ideas, the Twitterverse is a great place to get advice. Services such as Twoll or Pollowers allow you to set up a poll on your Twitter feed, which can be a great way to settle a friendly argument or decide on the best course of action for something.

ENHANCING YOUR CAREER

Although LinkedIn has become known as the professionals' social network, Twitter is still pretty useful for job searching and improving your career prospects. If you are looking for work, you can say so in your biography, as well as including a link to your CV. In addition, you can follow prospective employers and ask about any job vacancies by sending them a tweet.

Job Adverts

Many companies now tweet vacancies, thus making Twitter a really useful tool for finding a new job. Use hashtags such as #vacancy or #jobvacancy or services like TweetMyJobs.com to find out about the latest vacancies.

FUN AND GAMES

Twitter can also be a lot of fun. People play all sorts of games on it, from tweeting chess moves to one another to running Twitter contests and quizzes. It is also a great place for all sorts of creative projects, such as people tweeting a novel one sentence at a time or using the 140-character limit to create short stories.

Right: Twitter is a great place to find a job, follow potential employers and have fun playing games with friends.

TWITTER BASICS

ACCOUNT SETUP

If you are new to Twitter, before you can get tweeting, you need to set up an account. Thankfully, signing up to Twitter is relatively straightforward, but you will need a couple of things before you start.

TWITTER REQUIREMENTS

Anybody can set up a Twitter account. There is no particular age requirement, although Twitter say their services are 'not directed to persons under 13', and you do not need a credit or debit card. In fact, all that is really necessary is a valid email address, but you do have to come up with a username and password too.

- **Email address**: You can use any type of email address to set up a Twitter account.

- **Full name**: Twitter will ask for your name, but you do not have to use your own name if you do not wish to do so.

- **Username**: This will be your Twitter handle, which people will use when they mention or reply to you.

- **Password**: As with other internet activities, you need a password to protect your account.

WHAT NAME TO USE

Most of the people who use Twitter register using their real name. However, there are a couple of reasons why you may want to use another name for your Twitter account.

- **Business name**: If you are starting a Twitter account to promote your business and connect with customers, you may want to use your business name.

○ **Pseudonym:** Some people, such as authors using pen names, sign up to Twitter using a pseudonym, while others choose a different name because they wish to remain anonymous.

Verified Accounts

Many people in the public eye have found that other individuals are using their name and pretending to be them. In order to prevent this, Twitter contacts well-known people to verify their accounts and includes a blue tick next to the accounts which have been verified.

Above: Your username (handle) should reflect who you are or what you do, and be fewer than 15 characters.

YOUR TWITTER HANDLE

Your Twitter handle (username) is important, as it is what people will use when mentioning you in tweets or contacting you for a direct message. When using a handle on Twitter to mention or message somebody, you have to use the @ symbol before the username.

Choosing Your Username

Twitter will suggest a handle based on your full name. However, due to the sheer number of Twitter users already signed up, if you have a fairly common name, such as John Smith, you may find that this is already taken and Twitter will then suggest an alternative. This could be your name connected to a number of digits, e.g. John72812750, and may not be very memorable. Therefore, you may wish to come up with your own handle. However, try to think of something that is unique and make sure that your chosen username does not exceed 15 characters.

Hot Tip
If you decide that you do not like your Twitter handle, do not worry, as you can change it later, once you have signed up.

CHOOSING YOUR PASSWORD

Your password is important for keeping your Twitter account secure. A password needs to be at least eight characters, but it is recommended to use 10 and a mix of numbers and letters.

SETTING UP YOUR ACCOUNT

Once you have decided on what name, email account, username and password to use, it is time to sign up to your Twitter account. Thankfully, this is a straightforward process.

Step 2: Enter your full name, email address and password.

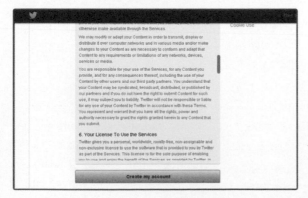

Step 6: Click the 'Create my account' button.

1. Visit twitter.com to begin the sign-up process.

2. In the box that says 'New to Twitter? Sign Up', enter your full name (or pseudonym or business name), email address and password.

3. Click the box that says 'Sign up for Twitter'.

4. On the next screen, Twitter will confirm whether your email address, name and password are okay (if an email is already in use, it will tell you).

5. Enter your chosen Twitter handle where it says 'Choose your username'.

6. Read the terms of service and then click the 'Create my account' button.

Above: Twitter will send you a confirmation email. Click 'Confirm your account now'.

Confirming Your Account

Once you have signed up to Twitter, you will need to confirm your account. In order to do this, Twitter will send you an email to the email address that you used in the sign-up process. Simply go to your inbox, open the email asking you to confirm your account and click the 'Confirm your account now' button. Alternatively, you can cut and paste the provided link into your browser.

Hot Tip

When choosing your Twitter password, do not pick the same one that you use for other internet activities because, if your Twitter account is compromised, then your other accounts could be at risk too.

GETTING STARTED

In order to get you started, Twitter will suggest popular people and friend recommendations for you to follow. Some of these recommendations may be taken directly from your email account address book. Some people do not like the way Twitter gains this sort of access to their personal information, but you can switch off this feature (*see* Settings, pp. 57–60).

THE TWITTER INTERFACE

When you have confirmed your account, you will be faced with the basic Twitter interface, where you can control your Twitter account, search for followers, send tweets or read what other people are tweeting.

NAVIGATIONAL BUTTONS

Along the top of the page, you will find several buttons, links and boxes, which are the basic navigational tools on Twitter.

Above: The Twitter interface allows you to control your account, search for followers, send tweets or read what other people are tweeting.

- **Home**: This takes you to your homepage, where you can see your tweets, followers and following statistics.

- **@ Connect**: This page lists any interactions you have had, such as mentions or people who have followed you.

- **# Discover**: This page has tools that make it easy for you to find people to follow, as well as showing you the most popular accounts.

- **Me**: Your profile page, which also shows your most recent tweets.

- **Search**: The search bar lets you search for people or subjects.

- **Direct message**: This button lets you send a direct message to somebody.

- **Settings**: Where you can alter your account settings.

- **Compose**: Opens the box for sending tweets.

> ## Hot Tip
> When you first sign up to Twitter, you may be surprised to see that you already have some followers. Normally, these are companies that pay to follow certain Twitter users when they sign up.

HOMEPAGE

Your Twitter homepage is where all the action takes place; here, you can send tweets and read what other people are tweeting about.

Compose Box

On the upper left-hand side of the homepage is the box where you can write your tweets. This is also where you can keep track of your tweets and followers, as around there you will see the following statistics:

- ▶ **Followers:** How many followers you have.

- ▶ **Following:** The number of people you are following.

- ▶ **Tweets:** How many tweets you have sent so far.

Above: The stats above the compose box show numbers of tweets, followers and people you're following.

Twitter Feed

By far the most prominent aspect of the homepage is the Twitter feed. This is where you can see all the tweets of the people you are following. Just like a blog, a Twitter feed is chronological, so the newest messages arrive at the top and push the older tweets down. When using the twitter.com interface, new tweets are hidden until you click the 'New Tweets' bar.

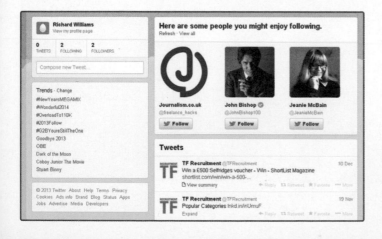

Trends

Below the compose box, you will see a list of links under the title 'Trends'. These are the most popular hashtags (*see* pages 103–105) and subjects being tweeted about in the Twittersphere.

Left: Trending topics are the most popular subjects being tweeted about at that moment.

@ CONNECT

The Connect page is where you connect with people. There are two main headings on this page:

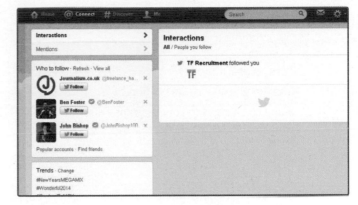

- **Interactions**: This Is where you can see who has followed you, who has retweeted your messages and if your tweets have been 'favorited' by anyone (*see* pages 150–152).

- **Mentions**: Here you can see the tweets that are replies to you or mention your Twitter handle.

Above: The Connect page Is where you see your interactions and mentions.

DISCOVER

The Discover page Is where you can find people to follow; there are several categories:

- **Tweets**: Tweets which may interest you, suggested by Twitter, based on your profile and followers.

- **Activity**: Who your followers are following, and what they are retweeting and marking as favorite.

- **Who to follow**: Recommended by Twitter for you, based on your followers and profile.

Above: The Discover page is designed to help you find other tweets and users you might find interesting.

○ **Find friends:** Where you can find people to follow.

○ **Popular accounts:** The most popular Twitter accounts.

ME

This is where you can see your profile and latest tweets. Note the button that says 'Edit profile'. This is where you can make changes to your biography and upload a picture (see pages 62–67).

(see pages 62–67).

SEARCH BAR

At the top of the page, Twitter has a search bar. This can be used for finding both people and subjects about which people are tweeting.

○ **People:** You can search for people either by typing in their real name or by using the @ symbol followed by their Twitter handle, e.g. @BarackObama.

○ **Subjects:** You can enter the name of any subject you want to read tweets about, but for more effective searching, you can use the hashtag (#) connected to the subject (see pages 103–105).

(see pages 103–105).

Left: The Me page displays your profile information as well as anything you have tweeted.

Hot Tip

When you make a search, Twitter will list the popular and recommended people and subjects based on your profile, followers and most popular searches.

SETTINGS

The settings menu lets you control your account and alter security and privacy settings, as well as making changes to your Twitter handle and contact information.

CHANGING YOUR SETTINGS

You can make all sorts of changes to your account settings by clicking the gearwheel symbol at the top right-hand side of your Twitter interface and select Settings. You will then be faced with a list of various options:

- **Account**: Where you can change your username (Twitter handle) and email address, and make other changes to your account.

- **Security and privacy**: Make changes to your security and privacy settings (see page 59).

- **Password**: Change your password.

- **Mobile**: Link your mobile phone to your Twitter account (see page 171).

- **Email notifications**: Receive notifications when somebody mentions, follows or retweets you.

Above: The Settings menu lets you control your account, alter security and privacy settings and make Twitter handle and contact information changes.

○ **Profile:** Change your biography and other profile information (*see* pages 61–65).

○ **Design:** Alter how your Twitter page looks (*see* pages 66–67)

○ **Apps:** Lists third-party applications that can access your account.

○ **Widgets:** Create widgets for you to use on your account (*see* pages 146–147 and 181).

> ## Hot Tip
> Twitter keeps all your information and all the tweets you have ever sent on file. You can request these at any time by clicking the 'Request your archive' button in Account settings.

ACCOUNT SETTINGS

You can change your username (Twitter handle), email address, language and time zone by altering them in the account settings panes. Remember that, when making any changes to your account settings, you have to click Save changes at the bottom of the page before any changes take effect.

Above: In account settings you can change your username, email address, language and time zone.

Content

In this section, Twitter lets you change your country of origin, as well as selecting whether or not you want to see tweets containing media that may be sensitive, such as nudity. In addition, a box lets you notify other users if your tweets contain sensitive material. Failing to tick this box could get your tweets sent for review if somebody flags them as inappropriate. If you select this option, users who have opted out of seeing sensitive media will have to click through a warning message before your tweets are revealed to them.

SECURITY AND PRIVACY

Twitter has a number of security and privacy settings, which include the following.

- **Tweet privacy**: If you check the 'Protect my Tweets' box, only your followers will be able to see your tweets. In addition, you will have to approve anybody who wishes to follow you, and your tweets will not be viewable in Google or other search engines.

- **Tweet location**: If you tick the 'Add a location to my Tweets' box, each tweet will show where you are when you send it. In this pane, you can also delete your location information from all tweets you have sent previously.

- **Discoverability**: By default, people can search for you by your email address; uncheck this box if you want to disable this feature.

- **Promoted content**: As with Facebook and other social networks, Twitter uses your personal details to tailor advertisements to you. However, you can opt out by unchecking the 'Promoted content' box.

- **Login verification**: This lets you make your Twitter account more secure. By selecting this feature, Twitter will send a verification code to your phone, either by SMS or via your Twitter app.

- **Password reset**: To reset your password you normally just need to enter your username, but with this feature checked, you will also have to enter your email address or phone number.

Hot Tip

You can add or remove your location in tweets by clicking the location button, which is below the compose box (next to the Add photo icon).

Above: Twitter has a number of settings to help protect your privacy.

Personalization

Twitter also suggests who you can follow using information gathered from websites you have visited recently that include a Twitter button or widget. Not every Twitter account will have this service available (it will depend on your browser settings), and you can disable it by unchecking the Personalization box in security and privacy settings.

Allowing Twitter Email Access

In addition to these security and privacy settings, Twitter has access to your email accounts and address books. Twitter uses this information to help you find people to follow, but you can allow or deny access to it.

1. Click the # Discover tab at the top of your Twitter interface and select 'Find friends.

2. Click the 'Search contacts' button next to your email accounts, enter your email login details, and then agree to allow access.

Step 2: You can grant Twitter access to your email account to connect you with people to follow.

3. To remove contacts, follow step 1, then click the link under the list of email providers. Click 'remove' and then confirm that's what you want to do.

OTHER SETTINGS

In the Settings menu, you can make all sorts of other changes to your Twitter account, such as adding a mobile phone number or selecting email notifications, as well as modifying the design of your Twitter page and adding your profile information. We'll go through many of these other settings throughout the rest of this book.

YOUR PROFILE

Your Twitter profile is how you tell the Twittersphere who you are. It is what will attract people to follow you, as well as explaining to people what you are about, so you need to make sure that you get it right.

YOUR TWITTER PROFILE

No matter what your motives are for joining Twitter, your profile is crucial for attracting followers. Not only should it be visible and as appealing to people as possible, but you may also want it to rank in search engine queries to help people find you, especially if you are using Twitter for business or promotion.

Profile Elements
Your Twitter profile has several elements to it:

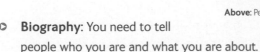

- **Name:** By now, you should have your name sorted.

- **Photo:** If you want to be noticed, a profile picture is essential.

Above: Personalize your profile by having a memorable name, profile picture and background.

- **Biography:** You need to tell people who you are and what you are about.

- **Location:** It doesn't have to be specific, but at least explain which country you reside in.

- **Background:** You want your profile page to look as appealing as possible.

CREATING YOUR PROFILE

In order to make changes to your profile, go into the Settings menu (in the drop-down menu under the gear wheel icon) and select Profile.

PHOTO AND HEADER

You can upload two types of image to your profile in Twitter:

Above: To change your profile photo or header, select Profile from the Settings menu.

- **Profile photo:** A picture of you, which allows users to put a face to your words.
- **Header:** This is a background image that you can use to individualize your profile page.

Your Profile Photo

People like to see who they are following and chatting to on Twitter. If you are setting up a Twitter account for a business, you may want to use your company logo as your profile image, but for everybody else, upload a picture of your face.

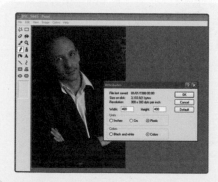

Hot Tip

Crop your profile picture to a size of 400 x 400 pixels. You can use any photo editing software to do this, but ensure that this is a high resolution image, otherwise it may appear blurred.

Uploading Your Profile Picture

1. Click 'Change photo' In the profile menu in Settings, then 'Upload photo'.

2. Choose the image you want to upload and click 'Open'.

3. By using the slider, you can make further adjustments to the position and size of your photo .

4. Click 'Apply' to install your photo to your profile page.

Step 2: Select the image to upload as your profile picture.

Step 3: Choose the best size and crop for your picture.

Your Header Image

Your header image is a background design for your profile that can help to individualize it. You can upload any sort of image, but try to choose something that represents you or about which you feel passionate. Alternatively, upload a pattern. You can upload the header image in the same way as your profile photo, by clicking 'Change header' in the profile menu in Settings. There are, however, a couple of things worth noting:

- **Size**: Try to use an image that is 1252 pixels wide by 626 pixels high, but you can only upload images up to 5 MB in size.

- **Format**: You can upload JPG, PNG and GIF formats.

Above: Upload an interesting header image by clicking 'Change header' in the profile menu in Settings.

YOUR TWITTER BIOGRAPHY

Just as crucial as your photograph is your biography, which is there to explain to people who you are. If you are a business or are using Twitter to promote something, use your biography to explain what it is that you do. If you are using Twitter as a social network to connect to people, then try to let your personality show in your biography. If you are setting up a Twitter account for a business or to promote something, it may be best to avoid being too jokey.

Bio-writing Tips

- **Size**: You have a little more space than in a tweet – but not much. Your bio has to fit into 160 characters, so it needs to be concise.

- **Who you are**: Think of words that explain to people who you are and what you do, such as 'musician', 'author' or even just 'mum'.

- **Search engine optimization**: If you are a business, insert a keyword or two in your biography so that search engines will find it.

ADDING LINKS TO YOUR PROFILE

Twitter allows you to place a URL to a website in your profile. If you are a business, make sure that you take advantage of this feature and insert your website address. If you are promoting books or music and don't have a website, then you should link to a website where your work is for sale. You can also use this URL to link to a blog or even another social networking site, such as your Facebook page.

Saving Your Profile

You can make changes to your profile at any time, but do not forget to click 'Save changes' after you have finished. Your changes will take effect immediately.

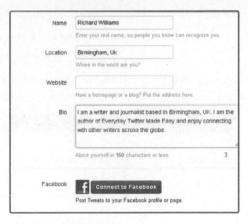

Above: You only have 160 characters to express yourself, so write a targeted bio.

Hot tip

You can make quick edits to your profile by clicking your name on the Twitter homepage and then clicking the 'Edit profile' button.

Above: You can click the 'Edit profile' button at any time to update your profile.

YOUR TWITTER DESIGN

You can further individualize and customize your profile page in the Design section in Settings. This is where you can make changes to the entire background of your Twitter page and further express yourself or reinforce your brand.

Above: Customize your background with different pictures and colours.

Background Themes

Twitter provides you with various themes that you can use to individualize your profile page. Setting a background theme is simple: just click on the one you like and your background will change (do not forget to apply it by clicking 'Save changes'). However, as these are available to everybody, you may wish to use your own design, especially if you are a business or are using Twitter to promote something.

Uploading Background Images

You can use any image as your background theme. Just click 'Change background' and upload an image or design of your own choosing. However, you can further customize it by using other options:

- **Tile background:** Instead of having the image spread across the whole page, ticking this box will tile the image multiple times.

- **Background position:** You can choose whether to centre your image or to justify it left or right.

Colours

You can further customize your background by changing the colours of your theme and profile page. You can do this to three aspects:

○ **Background**: If you like it but not its colour, simply change it by clicking 'Background color' and selecting a new one from the colour palette.

○ **Link color**: You can also change the colour of any links on your page and tweets.

○ **Overlay**: The overlay is a sort of shadow over your Twitter feed and profile that makes them easier to read. You can choose a black or white overlay.

Above: Your profile will be more memorable with colours and images tailored to you.

Your Last Tweets

Finally, when people click on your profile, they not only get to see your customized profile page, but also your last few tweets. This can help people to ascertain what sort of content you put out into the Twittersphere, so make sure that you do not leave any embarrassing or poorly written tweets lingering out there for too long.

JARGON BUSTING

When you first start using Twitter, all the abbreviations and symbols can make some tweets almost impossible to understand. In this chapter, we will try to decipher some of the most common jargon used on Twitter.

TWITTER SPEAK

As tweets are restricted to just 140 characters, Twitter users have developed their own type of language, known as Twitter Speak, so they can better communicate in such a short space. Twitter Speak makes use of a lot of abbreviations, symbols and shortenings, as well as some jargon that you will not find outside of the Twittersphere.

Above: The @ sign before another user's name means they will see your message. The # symbol marks a keyword in the tweet.

TWITTER SYMBOLS

Symbols are used quite frequently on Twitter, but they are more than just abbreviations; they serve some important functions.

- **@:** The @ sign is used to communicate with other Twitter users. If you place the sign before a person's Twitter handle, your tweet will appear in their Twitter feed.

- **#:** The hash symbol is placed before keywords, topics and events to turn them into hashtags. Including a # sign turns a word into a clickable hashtag (*see* pages 103–105).

Hot Tip

You may occasionally come across the @ and # signs used in general speak, such as 'I'm @ home' or 'Her album is # 4'. These are just shortenings for 'at' (@) and 'number' (#).

Other Symbols

While less common, you will occasionally come across a couple of other symbols in the Twittersphere too.

- ∧ : Often found at the end of a tweet, the hat sign is used to denote a tweet sent by an individual on behalf of a shared account. It is usually followed by a person's initials.

- $: Used to denote a financial entity. It works similarly to hashtags and is used before a company's stock market abbreviation; it will turn the name into a link.

TWITTER TERMINOLOGY

Twitter is full of its own jargon, and knowing what these words mean is crucial for understanding the platform.

- **Retweet**: When you forward somebody else's tweet to all your followers.

- **Tweet**: A Twitter message.

- **Feed**: Your Twitter feed is where you see the tweets sent by those you are following.

Right: The Twitter feed is updated every time someone you follow writes a new tweet.

- **Followers**: People who receive your tweets.

- **Following**: People whose tweets you receive in your feed.

- **Mention**: When somebody mentions your Twitter handle in a tweet, preceded by the @ sign.

- **Twitter handle**: Your Twitter username.

- **Hashtag**: A topic or keyword preceded by a # sign that is linkable and searchable, allowing you to find tweets on the same words.

- **Trending**: Topics that are currently the most popular on Twitter.

- **Tailored topic**: Topics tailored to you by Twitter based on your profile and subjects you commonly discuss.

- **Twerp**: A fool or twit ,specifically on Twitter someone who uses stupid or insulting tweets against better-known individuals in order to try and attract their followers.

TWITTER ABBREVIATIONS

Since 140 characters are not much in which to get your point across, Twitter users often resort to abbreviations. These can be bewildering for those new to Twitter, but once you understand them, you will be able to tweet more concisely.

- **RT**: A retweet.

- **AFAIK**: As far as I know.

- **CC**: Carbon copy. Used in a similar way as in emails, it helps to ensure that somebody gets a message.

- **CX**: Correction.

- **DM**: Direct message.

- **#FF**: Follow Friday – a Twitter custom where people suggest individuals to follow on Fridays.

- **HT**: Hat tip – to suggest respect, i.e. tipping one's hat.

- **ICYMI**: In case you missed it (often sent with a repeated tweet).

- **LOL**: Laughing out loud – to suggest that you find something funny.

- **#MM**: Music Monday – another Twitter tradition when people recommend bands or artists to each other.

- **MT or MRT**: Modified tweet – usually a retweet that has been edited.

- **NSFW**: Not safe for work – usually a link to some inappropriate content that should only be viewed at home.

- **SMH**: Shaking my head – used to suggest bewilderment.

- **TFTF**: Thanks for the follow.

- **TLDR**: Too long, didn't read – to suggest that you didn't have time to read something.

- **TMB**: Tweet me back.

- **TQRT**: Thanks for the retweet.

- **TT**: A translated tweet.

- **W/**: Short for 'with'.

Hot Tip

If you come across an abbreviation that you do not understand, do not be afraid to ask. Most Twitter users will be more than happy to explain it to you.

PLATFORMS

One of the great things about Twitter is its versatility. You can use it on your computer, your phone or tablet, as well as taking advantage of the various apps and programs that can help to maximize your Twitter experience.

INTERACTING WITH TWITTER

For most people new to Twitter, using the website at twitter.com on a regular internet browser is the simplest and easiest way to get accustomed to it. However, there are numerous ways of interacting with Twitter, and you may find that you prefer using a third-party client or app to help manage your Twitter account (see page 170), or you may choose the freedom of being able to send and receive tweets anywhere by using a phone or tablet.

Above: twitter.com is the browser version of Twitter.

INTERNET BROWSERS

You can access Twitter on any desktop computer or laptop with an internet connection. Twitter is compatible with all the main browsers, such as Internet Explorer, Firefox and Chrome. Using Twitter in this way does have some advantages over third-party apps, or using Twitter on your phone or tablet.

Above: You can see other people's profile designs on twitter.com, but not on all other platforms.

Advantages of Accessing Twitter on the Internet

○ **Simplicity:** As the interface on twitter.com is straightforward to use, sending tweets, retweeting and finding people to follow is simple.

○ **Speed:** Many apps only retrieve messages at set intervals, meaning there may be a delay before you receive a tweet or message. Sending and receiving using an internet browser is instant.

○ **Data limits:** If you are using a phone or tablet app, you may be tied to a data limit, which could prevent you from using Twitter if you hit that limit. In addition, third-party clients are restricted by API limits that affect how frequently they can access Twitter (see page 243 for more information).

○ **Functionality:** The Twitter website allows more functionality. For instance, users can send a tweet with the click of one button, but many apps do not allow this function.

○ **Profile backgrounds:** When using a desktop app (often called a client) or even some phone apps, you may not be able to view other users' profile backgrounds.

○ **Information:** twitter.com as viewed on an internet browser also offers more easily accessible information, such as trending topics and recommendations.

Hot Tip

If you want to access more than one Twitter account using an internet browser, you can use the private browsing function, which will allow you to log on to a second account.

Disadvantages of Accessing Twitter on the Internet

Despite its many advantages, the reason so many people use desktop and phone apps instead of accessing twitter.com over the internet is that it does have some flaws:

- **Tied to a desktop**: These days, we are as likely to access Twitter on a phone or tablet as we are a desktop computer or laptop. Having the freedom to access Twitter on the go is a distinct advantage of phone apps.

- **Management**: It is difficult to filter tweets and followers using an internet browser. Twitter apps enable greater management of your followers and tweets.

- **Groups**: Although you can create lists on twitter.com so you can see selected tweets, you cannot create group-specific messages; however, Twitter apps allow this.

- **Multiple accounts**: Unless you open a separate private browsing window or use another browser, you can only log on to one account at twitter.com, but some desktop apps let you run multiple accounts and even send all tweets to one feed.

Above: The mobile version of Twitter makes it easy to send and receive tweets on the go.

TWITTER ON THE GO

One of the distinct advantages of Twitter over other social networks is that it is incredibly easy to send and receive tweets using a mobile device. You can either use the mobile browser version at mobile.twitter.com or get free Twitter apps for all major smartphone and tablet operating systems.

○ **Twitter on iOS**: iPhone and iPad users can download the Twitter app from the App Store (itunes.apple.com).

○ **Twitter on Android**: The Google Play store (play.google.com) carries the latest Twitter app for Android devices.

○ **Twitter on Windows phones**: For Windows phones and tablets, download the Twitter app from the Windows Phone store (windowsphone.com).

Using Phone and Tablet Apps

Using an app on a phone or tablet is a little easier than trying to access Twitter mobile. The apps are designed to be simpler to use on a hand-held device, so you do not have to enlarge sections of the screen or flick between pages. You can also receive notifications on your phone's screen.

Above: Apps are designed for easy use on a hand-held device; for Android devices, you can download the app from Google Play.

Twitter Texts

While most people use smartphones these days, you can still send tweets using SMS (short message service) text messages (*see* pages 171–173). Twitter was originally designed for this function, which is why tweets are only 140 characters (the length of an SMS message – 160 characters – minus 20 characters that Twitter requires for a user's handle.). To send SMS tweets, you will first have to create a Twitter account via SMS (for more information on how to do this, *see* pages 166–173).

TWITTER MANAGEMENT APPS

Twitter desktop apps, also known as Twitter clients, are programs designed to help you to manage your Twitter account. Many of these apps offer added functionality and customization compared to the basic Twitter interface (for more detail on using Twitter clients, *see* pages 174–178).

Some of the most popular Twitter clients include the following:

Above: Apps like TweetDeck make it easy to manage your account from one interface.

- **TweetDeck:** Twitter's own desktop client, which is free to download.

- **HootSuite:** One of the most popular clients that lets you manage all your social media accounts in one place.

- **Tweetings:** One of the most feature-packed clients; it is free on Windows, but you have to pay for use on Android or Apple devices.

LISTS

When you start building up followers, you may wonder how you can keep track of everybody, or separate those more important tweets from the general background noise. The answer is to create lists.

TWITTER LISTS

Creating Twitter lists enables you to group a number of followers together. This will allow you to categorize them into groups, such as friends, colleagues, information accounts, etc. By creating lists, you can see tweets from a specific group without having to search your entire Twitter feed.

Reasons to Create Lists

- **Categorize people:** You can categorize people by their expertise or occupation, which is useful if you are using Twitter to connect with people in your industry.

- **Work/Social:** You can separate tweets from your friends from those for work.

- **Visibility:** You can make your list visible so that other people can share contacts with other Twitter users.

Above: Categorize your followers into different lists; this means you'll be able to see tweets from certain groups of people without having to search your feed.

○ **Management:** Lists make it easier to manage your Twitter feed, as you can see specific tweets from those in a certain list.

List Restrictions

Creating lists on Twitter used to be really restrictive, as you could only have 20 lists with just 500 accounts on each list. However, recent changes mean that you can now make up to 1,000 lists, each containing as many as 5,000 accounts. The big constraint with Twitter lists, however, is that you can only use them for reading tweets and not for sending them just to list members.

Public or Private

When you create a list, you can choose whether to make it public or keep it private. With a public list, other Twitter users can follow it. In addition, if your list is public, everybody placed on it receives a notification, which can prompt people to follow you. However, you may wish to create private lists, such as grouping your friends together, and Twitter allows this too.

List Names

When you create a list, you need to give it a name. However, avoid being too generic and think of specific list names, so that when people find your list, they identify exactly the type of people who are on it. List names have to be fewer than 25 characters.

CREATING A TWITTER LIST

1. Click the Settings menu (gear wheel icon); select Lists in the drop-down menu and then click 'Create list'.

2. Enter a name for your list, a brief description and whether you want the list to be public or private.

3. Click 'Save list'.

Step 2: Type a name and description for your new list to help identify it.

Adding and Removing People from Lists

You can add anybody to a list – even those people you are not following.

1. In order to add or remove somebody from a list, visit their profile page by clicking their username and then click their name on the profile summary pop-up.

2. Access the drop-down menu from the gear icon and click 'Add or remove from lists'.

3. Your created lists will appear in a pop-up. Tick to which list you would like to add the person or uncheck if you want to remove them.

Left: To access your lists, go to your profile (or Me) page and select Lists from the bottom of the left-hand menu.

Viewing List Members

In order to view members on your list, go to your profile page, select 'Lists' in the Settings menu, click the List name, then 'List members'.

Step 2: Select a list to see tweets from members of that list only.

FILTERING YOUR TWITTER FEED

The big advantage of creating lists is that you can filter your Twitter feed to display only tweets from list members.

1. Go to your profile page and click on the 'Lists' link in the left-hand menu.

2. Click the list from which you want to see tweets.

3. A timeline of tweets will appear from users in that list.

Editing and Deleting Lists

1. If you want to edit or delete a list, click 'Lists' on the drop-down menu beside the Settings gear icon at the top of the page.

2. Select which list you'd like to edit or delete.

Hot Tip

To see which public lists other users have placed you in, click the Settings icon (gear wheel), go to your Lists page and click on 'Member of'.

3. Click 'Edit' to make changes to your list details, such as the name or description, or click 'Delete' to remove the list.

Subscribing to Lists

If you are unsure about what type of lists to create, you can follow other people's Twitter lists and try them out to see if they are helpful. You do not need to be following someone to subscribe to one of their lists and you can unsubscribe at any time.

1. In order to see what lists other people are following, visit their profile page by clicking their username and then click their name on the profile summary pop-up. Select Lists from the side menu.

2. If you want to follow a list, simply select it and click 'Subscribe'.

Sharing Lists

You can also share lists with your followers. Simply copy the URL (web address) of the list you would like to share and paste it into a tweet or direct message.

Above: Copy the web address of your chosen list and paste into a tweet or message to share it with others.

THE TWEET

COMPOSING YOUR TWEET

Once you have signed up to Twitter and created your profile, it is time to send your first tweet. This can be daunting. After all, what on earth do you say? And how do you actually compose and send it?

THE COMPOSE BOX

When you send a tweet, you write it in the compose box, which can be accessed in two ways. You can either click the box on the left of your Twitter homepage, where it says 'Compose new tweet' or you can click the blue icon on the top right-hand side (the one that looks like a quill), which can be clicked no matter which page you are on.

Above: The number of characters in your tweet will appear at the bottom right of the compose box; if it turns red, you have exceeded 140 characters.

Character Counter

Since all tweets have to be fewer than 140 characters, the compose box contains a counter on the bottom right. This starts at 140 and if you exceed the limit, it turns red and will have a minus sign, showing how many characters you have exceeded the limit by. In some browsers, the excess characters will also be highlighted.

WHAT TO TWEET ABOUT

Perhaps the most challenging aspect of Twitter for a new user is knowing what to say. The first few tweets are always the hardest, but once you start tweeting, it soon becomes second nature.

The great thing about Twitter is you can say almost anything. Here are some ideas.

- ○ **Introduce yourself**: For your first tweet, why not introduce yourself to the Twittersphere?

- ○ **News**: Comment on something interesting that you have seen in the news.

- ○ **Entertainment**: Tweet about a film you have seen, book you have read or album you have listened to.

Above: It is a good idea to introduce yourself in your first ever tweet.

Before you start tweeting, you could retweet what other people have been saying so that you can get used to Twitter and also introduce yourself slowly to the Twittersphere.

- ○ **What you are doing**: If you are doing something interesting, let the Twittersphere know.

- ○ **Send a link**: Link to something interesting you have seen on the internet.

CRAMMING IT ALL IN

The most challenging aspect of tweeting for beginners is getting down what you want to say in just 140 characters. In order to tweet successfully, you need to learn how to write concisely and edit your tweets until they are the right length.

Tweet Editing

Perhaps the simplest way to learn how to edit down a tweet is to write out exactly what you want to say, ignoring the 140-character rule, and then go back and cut down your text so that it fits.

Above: There are various tricks to shorten the number of characters you use.

- **Abbreviations:** Use common abbreviations where possible.

- **Symbols:** Use common symbols, such as '&' instead of 'and'.

- **Cut:** Remove extraneous words, such as adverbs and modifiers. Instead of saying: 'This website is very interesting' just write 'This website is interesting'.

- **Organize:** Rejig your sentences so that they use as few words as possible.

- **Spaces:** Try removing spaces after commas and stops.

- **Word length:** See if you can use a shorter word instead of a longer one.

- **Twitter Speak:** Learn the common Twitter phrases and abbreviations to save space.

SENDING YOUR FIRST TWEET

That first tweet can be the most daunting, but once it is out of the way, you will be surprised at how quickly you get accustomed to talking to the Twittersphere. Additionally, sending a tweet is incredibly simple:

1. Click the compose box and type in what you want to say.

2. If necessary, edit down your tweet until the character counter turns black and is not showing minus numbers.

3. Press 'Tweet'. Your tweet is now live.

Step 3: When ready to post your message, press the Tweet button.

LOCATION-BASED TWEETS

Twitter has a feature that allows you to add your location to your tweets. Although it can be a good idea to let people know where you are if you are travelling around or communicating to people in other countries, you may not want to broadcast your location if you are away from home and your house is empty.

Step 2: Click the location icon.

TURNING TWEET LOCATION ON AND OFF

You can set your tweet location on and off in your settings (see Chapter Two), but also in individual tweets.

1. Compose your tweet as normal.

2. Click the pin-shaped location icon next to the camera icon on the bottom of the compose box.

3. A box will appear asking whether you want to include a location in your tweets. Press the blue 'Turn location on' or click the 'Not now' link.

4. Send tweet as normal.

DELETING A TWEET

When you send a tweet, it is visible for the whole world to see, but if for some reason you wish to remove it from the Twittersphere, you can. Remember, however, that you cannot delete tweets that other people have retweeted.

Step 3: Press the 'Turn location on' button to add a location to your tweets.

1. Click 'Tweets' on the top left of the compose box.

2. Find the tweet that you want to delete.

3. Hover your mouse pointer on the tweet and click the Delete link when it appears.

Step 3: Click Delete to erase a tweet.

PROTECTING YOUR TWEETS

When you send a tweet, it is not just your followers who get to see it; anybody can find it in a search, retweet it and spread it around the Twittersphere. This means that a tweet can reach thousands and even millions of individuals. However, some people just wish to use Twitter as a place to connect with their friends and do not want their messages visible to the entire world. Twitter enables you to protect tweets so that only your followers can see them.

Making Your Tweets Private

1. Go into your Security and Privacy settings (click the gear wheel icon, select Settings and click 'Security and privacy').

2. In the 'Tweet privacy' section, tick the box beside 'Protect my Tweets'.

3. Click 'Save changes' at the bottom of the page. Twitter will usually ask for your password to confirm the changes.

Step 1: Click the gear wheel icon and select Settings.

Hot Tip

If you protect your tweets, your followers cannot retweet them, and anybody who wants to follow you or see your messages will need your approval first.

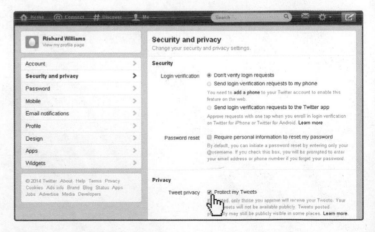

Step 2: Tick the 'Protect my Tweets' box.

SETTING THE TONE

No matter why you have joined Twitter, you need to ensure that you are creating the right impression if you want to gain followers. This means setting the right tone when you are tweeting and addressing the Twittersphere.

SPEAKING TO THE WORLD

As it is so easy to send a tweet, it is also easy to forget that the entire Twitter community can see it. Twitter offers people confidence, allowing even normally shy individuals to express themselves and offer their opinions on subjects they feel passionate about. However, this has led many people to declare things on Twitter that they would not normally say.

Tweeting as Publishing

Perhaps the most important thing to remember about Twitter is that tweeting is publishing. In other words, what you say is visible for the whole world to see. Just as with other forms of publishing, this means that you need to take care with what you say and how you say it. Not only can you run into legal issues (*see* pages 226–34 for more details), but it is also easy to offend people or come across in a way that you did not intend.

Language and Content

When tweeting, it is important to think about your choice of language. Since you will not know all your followers personally, it is very easy to offend people with the language and content of your tweets.

YOUR TWITTER PERSONA

Few of your followers will actually know who you are away from Twitter. How people perceive you is all down to your Twitter persona, and it is this above all else that will attract followers.

Hot Tip

Avoid using swearwords in your tweets, and refrain from writing anything that other people may perceive as offensive.

- **Tone:** Try to ensure that you keep the tone of your tweets friendly. Being too confrontational or aggressive may put people off following you.

Richard Williams
View my profile page

1	2	1
TWEET	FOLLOWING	FOLLOWER

I am so @#@@# annoyed at the moment.

104   Tweet

- **Personality:** Try to let your personality shine through in your tweets, which is no easy task in just 140 characters. However, do not say something on Twitter that you would not say in real life.

- **Consistency:** Be consistent. If people expect you to send a certain type of tweet and in a certain tone, changing from the norm can lose you followers.

Left: Avoid offensive language in your tweets by using symbols instead of swearwords.

PROMOTION AND BUSINESS TWEETS

Setting the right tone is crucial for those using Twitter for promotion. Your Twitter persona will reflect on your business, so you need to ensure that you keep it as professional as possible.

The Professional Tweet

For the professional tweeter, the tone of your tweets is crucial.

- **Negativity:** Twitter allows customers to communicate with you directly. Avoid getting into arguments or responding in an aggressive or overly defensive manner to complaints.

Above: Many companies use Twitter to address customer concerns and complaints.

- **Be professional**: Do not talk badly about your customers, even anonymously. Saying things like: 'I have just spoken to the customer from hell' will give a bad impression to other customers.

- **Address concerns**: Twitter gives you the opportunity to search for tweets about your company or products. Take advantage of it, and if you find negative comments or complaints, try to respond directly to the tweeter and put things right by addressing their concerns.

- **Be transparent**: Be open on Twitter. Reveal as much information about your company as possible. Twitter is about engagement and openness, so answer people's questions and do not hide away.

WHEN AND HOW MUCH TO TWEET

Some people tweet dozens of times a day, whereas others only tweet once or twice a week. Knowing how often to tweet can be difficult to work out, especially if you are new to the Twittersphere.

HOW OFTEN TO TWEET

The great thing about Twitter is how accessible it is: you can tweet wherever you are and whenever you like. You do not have to be tied to your desk to interact with the Twitterverse, so if you have something to say, you can tweet it by using your smartphone or tablet. However, it is also easy to overdo it, and some people tweet relentlessly.

Content is King

If the content of your messages is always good, then there is no limit to how often you should tweet, but there is little point in tweeting just for the sake of it. Perhaps the golden rule for knowing how much to tweet is only to use Twitter when you have something to say.

Tweet Frequency

How often you tweet can also depend on whether you are an individual or a business.

Right: Only tweet when you have something to say; try to avoid banal messages.

Richard Williams
View my profile page

1	2	1
TWEET	FOLLOWING	FOLLOWER

One more hour until lunch time.

109   Tweet

Trends · Change
#Merkel

- **Business tweets**: People may perceive you as sending out spam if you tweet too often. Avoid sending more than 10 tweets a day if you are promoting or running a business, unless you are replying to individuals.

- **Individuals**: As long as you have something to say, tweet as often as you like, but avoid boring people with banal tweets.

Hot Tip

As a beginner, try to send at least three or four tweets a day, so that people will get to know you.

WHEN TO TWEET

You can tweet at any time of day. However, because of the amount of activity on Twitter, it is very easy for your messages to become buried, especially if your followers are not around when you write. Therefore, try to time your tweets for when your followers are most active. For instance, if you use Twitter to connect with people at work, write during working hours, while early evening is perhaps the best time to connect with friends and socialize. It is also worth noting what country and time zone your followers are in.

Overdoing It

One thing that can put off followers is if you put out too many tweets which lack content. Filling up people's Twitter feed with banal messages will just frustrate people, so ensure that you are not overdoing it.

Serial Tweeters

Some Twitter users send tweets every few minutes, but often these messages contain nothing more than idle chat or updates on what they are doing. However, few people are interested in what you are eating for lunch or what your cat is up to. Only tweet what you think people will be interested in reading.

Repeating Tweets

It is fine to repeat a tweet that you have already sent. After all, it is very easy for tweets to become buried. However, avoid sending out the same message more than two or three times. In addition, send out repeated tweets at a different time of day, thus ensuring that you have the best chance of people seeing them. This is especially important if you have followers in different countries and time zones. It is also a good idea to let people know if a tweet is repeated.

Right: Indicate that you are repeating a tweet by including the phrase 'ICYMI' (in case you missed it).

KEEPING YOUR TWEETS INTERESTING

Whatever and whenever you tweet, the secret to gaining followers and obtaining retweets is to ensure that you are only providing good-quality content. With just 140 characters to play with, writing engaging tweets can be a challenge – and it takes time and practice to get it right – but there are some ways to ensure that you will be sending the best tweets possible:

> **Hot Tip**
>
> Tweet about what matters to you. If you are passionate about something, your enthusiasm will shine through in your tweets; therefore, avoid talking about things in which you have little interest.

- **Originality:** Be original. Try to tweet things that haven't already been tweeted by other people or find interesting angles on articles for discussion.

- **Short and punchy:** Even though you have 140 characters to play with, you do not have to use them all. Think of a tweet as if it were a headline: keep it succinct and to the point.

Above: Include links to interesting or useful websites in your tweets.

- **Value:** Things that provide useful information are more likely to be retweeted than simple observations.

- **Links:** Send people links to useful information and articles (*see* pages 106–110)

- **Space:** Allow enough space for other users to comment and/or assign your username if they manually retweet a message.

RETWEETS, REPLIES AND MENTIONS

You will be able to gauge how well you are doing on Twitter by looking at the number of retweets, mentions and replies you receive. Learning how to retweet, reply and mention other users is a crucial aspect of interacting on Twitter.

WHAT IS A RETWEET?

In simple terms, a retweet is when somebody forwards your tweet. Unlike forwarding an email to another person, retweets are sent on to all your followers. These people may also retweet your tweet, thus meaning that hundreds, thousands or even millions of people could see your message – and the more retweets a tweet receives, the more people will get to see it.

Due to the exposure that a retweet offers, they have become the most sought-after feature on Twitter. Even long-term Twitter users still get excited when they get retweets, but it can be difficult to acquire them, especially if you are new to the platform.

Right. Retweets appear in your Twitter feed with the original author's name.

> ⎘ View details   ← Reply   ⇄ Retweet   ★ Favorite   ••• More
>
> **Ed Coburn** @EdwardJCoburn   30m
> I love your tweets :) said @HayleyLugassy about the quotes Ed Coburn sends out.
> ⇄ Retweeted by Jeff Joseph Author
> Expand   ← Reply   ⇄ Retweet   ★ Favorite   ••• More
>
> **Doris-Maria Heilmann** @111publishing   30m
> Bestseller Author Stephen King – King of Business Stephen King's business success, which is stemming
> pinterest.com/pin/2620532720…
> ⇄ Retweeted by Jeff Joseph Author
> Expand   ← Reply   ⇄ Retweet   ★ Favorite   ••• More
>
> **Daniel Kemp** @danielkemp6   31m
> "I'M HOT, I WANT A BATH AND I WANT YOU!" Not a story about sex, but there's enough of it in the story. dld.bz/ddsKt
> ⇄ Retweeted by Jeff Joseph Author
> Expand   ← Reply   ⇄ Retweet   ★ Favorite   ••• More

Above: The Retweet icon.

Retweets in Your Twitter Feed

Retweets appear in your Twitter feed and look the same as regular tweets, except for the fact that, apart from the original author's name and username, they also display a retweet icon (this looks a bit like a recycling logo) and the words 'Retweeted by' followed by the name of the Twitter user who retweeted them.

You will see the following three types of retweets in your Twitter feed:

- **Your tweets:** Any tweet you have sent that is retweeted.

- **Your retweets:** Any other user's tweets that you have retweeted.

- **People you follow:** Any tweet that has been retweeted by someone you follow you will see in your feed.

RETWEETING A TWEET

You can retweet anybody's tweet, as long as it isn't protected. This means that you can retweet somebody's message even if you are not following that person. Retweeting is incredibly simple.

Step 2: Click the Retweet button to confirm.

1. Select the message you want to forward to all your followers and click the Retweet link.

2. Twitter will ask you to confirm your retweet in a pop-up box. Just click the Retweet button.

TURNING OFF A PERSON'S RETWEETS

Occasionally, somebody you follow will retweet a lot of messages which don't interest you. Rather than unfollowing that user, you can simply turn off their retweets, meaning that you will only see that person's tweets and not what they have retweeted.

1. Go to the user's profile by clicking their username.

2. Click the person's icon next to the Following button.

3. Select 'Turn off Retweets' from the drop-down menu.

Step 3: If you follow someone who retweets too much, go to their profile and select 'Turn off Retweets'.

HOW TO GET RETWEETS

If you want to reach as wide an audience as possible, you will need to get retweets for your messages. Although many people new to Twitter find that they can be fairly elusive, there are a few things you can do to maximize your chances of getting them.

- **Content**: People are only going to retweet things that are worth sharing with their followers, so make sure that you are putting out great content.

- **Retweet others**: If you retweet things that other people are saying, they are more likely to reciprocate and retweet one of your messages.

Above: Manually retweeting a message allows you to modify or add to it.

- **Compose**: Make sure that your tweets are retweet-friendly. Try to leave a little room in case a user wants to add a comment or modify the retweet.

REPLIES

When you tweet, you may find that people will reply to what you have written. Replies enable people to use Twitter in order to strike up conversations and discussions. Twitter lets you see entire conversations by clicking the 'View conversation' link at the bottom of a replied tweet. If you are

not following a user and they reply to a tweet that you have sent, this will not appear In your Twitter feed, but you can see it on your Mentions tab on the @ Connect page.

Replying to a Tweet

Replying to a tweet is simple. If more than one person is engaged in the conversation, you can reply to all of them. You can also add other users to the conversation or remove existing ones.

1. Click the Reply link on the tweet to which you want to reply.

2. A compose box will appear, containing the handle of the person who originally tweeted. You can remove a user's handle or add others.

3. Compose your reply and click Tweet.

Step 3: Click the Reply link and compose your message.

MENTIONS

Twitter also enables you to mention users in tweets, thus letting you strike up conversations. When you mention somebody, he or she will receive your tweet in their Mention tab on their @ Connect page, even if you do not follow them. Followers will see any mentions in their main Twitter feed.

Hot Tip

You can use the notifications settings in Twitter to alert you by email whenever you get a retweet, a reply or a mention.

Mentioning a Twitter User

In order to mention somebody, simply include their Twitter handle in your tweet (remembering to add the @ symbol before it). You can mention as many people as you like in a tweet (as long as you do not exceed 140 characters), and clicking on any of their names will take you to their profile page.

Interactions

All / People you follow

🐦 **TheReal Mark Cassell** and 4 others followed you   4 Jan

🔁 **Monica Gloria, Rhea and Rory James** and **Jay Scully**   21 Nov
retweeted a Tweet you were mentioned in
20 Nov: #ww These writers followback writers (#1) @ForresterRobert
@MGEdwardsWrites @KathleenPalm @RheaRoryJames #writing

⭐ **Monica Gloria** and **Rhea and Rory James** favorited a Tweet   21 Nov
you were mentioned in
20 Nov: #ww These writers followback writers (#1) @ForresterRobert
@MGEdwardsWrites @KathleenPalm @RheaRoryJames #writing

Above: The Interactions page allows you to track when you have been mentioned or your messages have been retweeted or favorited.

TRACKING YOUR RETWEETS, MENTIONS AND REPLIES

If you want to know who and what is being retweeted, visit the @ Connect page on your Twitter interface. Here you will see all your messages that have been retweeted, as well as all your mentions and replies.

HASHTAGS

The hashtag is one of the most useful features on Twitter. Hashtags let you find topics of interest, as well as helping you to categorize your tweets, but some people find them confusing at first.

WHAT IS THE HASHTAG?

The hashtag is unique to Twitter and, simply put, is a keyword preceded by the # symbol. Hashtags have several uses, and learning how to implement them can help you to maximize your Twitter experience.

Hot Tip

Hashtags can occur anywhere in a tweet and you can include as many as you like.

- **Categorizing tweets:** You can use hashtags to categorize a tweet in order to make it easy for people to find it in Twitter searches.

- **Linking:** When you attach a hashtag to a word, it becomes a clickable link that will take users to a page listing all other tweets marked with the same hashtag.

- **Trends:** Hashtags help Twitter to compile a list of the most popular subjects being discussed at any one time, which are known as trending topics.

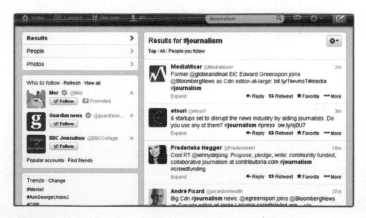

Above: Clicking on a word with a hashtag in front will take you to a page listing of other tweets marked with the same hashtag.

Creating a Hashtag

In order to create a hashtag, all you have to do is include the # symbol before any word (with no space). Once a hashtag is included, anybody can find the tweet by doing a Twitter search for it.

FINDING RELEVANT HASHTAGS

Hashtags have been around for a while and therefore, no matter what topic you are tweeting about, there is probably a hashtag already in existence for it. It is always worth doing a little research to find out which hashtags are connected to the subject about which you are tweeting. You can use services such as hashtags.org and TweetChat.com to find existing hashtags.

Some common types of hashtag include the following:

- **Events**: Most events and conferences will have a hashtag assigned to them, such as #digitalexpo2014.

- **Products**: If you are tweeting about a product, it can be useful to hashtag the name, such as #microsoftword.

- **Quotes**: If you are quoting somebody famous, use the hashtag #quote.

- **Entertainment**: Use #book, #film or #music when discussing types of entertainment.

- **Industry**: Most industries have hashtags, such as #journalism, #retail or #IT.

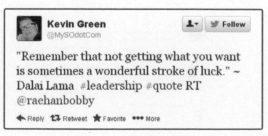

Kevin Green
@MySOdotCom

🔽 ▾   🐦 Follow

"Remember that not getting what you want is sometimes a wonderful stroke of luck." ~ Dalai Lama #leadership #quote RT @raehanbobby

↩ Reply   ↻ Retweet   ★ Favorite   ••• More

Above: The #quote hashtag is commonly used when quoting somebody famous.

TRENDING TOPICS

Trending topics appear on the left-hand side of the Home, @ Connect and # Discover pages on Twitter, and they help you to identify which subjects are the most popular at the moment. However, trends are user-specific: Twitter provides trending

Above: A list of trending topics appears on the left-hand side of the page.

information depending on who you follow and where you are based. Many trending topics are based on hashtags, and the full hashtag is listed in Trends; some subjects do not have hashtags but have become popular enough keywords to become trending topics.

Customizing Trends

You can change your trending topics by changing your chosen location.

1. Click 'Change' at the top of the Trends box, then select 'Change' in the pop-up box.

2. Select a new location from the menu or use the search box.

3. Click 'Done' to receive trends based on the new location.

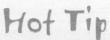

Hot Tip

Although you can include as many hashtags as you like in a tweet, do not overdo it. Tweets with too many hashtags can look like spam.

Above: You will see different trending topics if you change your location.

LINKS, IMAGES AND VIDEOS

In order to enhance your tweets, you can include images, videos or links to other websites or messages. These can help to make the tweets you put out far more interesting to your followers and increase the likelihood of you getting retweets and more follows.

LINKS IN TWEETS

Twitter is a great platform for sharing links and showing other people what you have seen on the internet. Tweets containing links are far more likely to get noticed than those with just plain text. You can link in two ways on Twitter:

- **External websites:** You can post a link to anything you like, including websites or other social media pages.

- **Tweets:** Each tweet has its own URL. In order to link to a tweet, simply click the Twitter handle of the person who sent it and then click Details to be taken to the tweet's own page, where you can copy and paste its URL.

Left: Tweets which include links are more likely to get interest from other users.

TWEETING LINKS

In order to include a link in a tweet, simply paste or type it into the compose box. Twitter will automatically turn the link live, allowing people to click it when you send the tweet. However, Twitter never displays the full URL in a tweet.

Hot Tip

Twitter automatically shortens links to 22 characters using its own link-shortening service: http://t.co – no matter how long they are.

LINK SHORTENING

Since you only have 140 characters in a tweet, several long links would take up valuable room. For this reason, you can also use various other services to shorten a URL. These smaller links will still take users to the desired website.

- **bitly.com**: Will shorten links to just 14 characters.

- **tiny.cc**: Also shortens links to 14 characters.

- **ow.ly/url/shorten-url**: Shortens links to 18 characters.

Step 2: Paste the link into the box.

How to Shorten a Link

1. Visit one of the link-shortening services mentioned above.

2. Paste your full-length link into the link box.

3. Click the button next to the box to shorten it.

4. Copy and paste the supplied shortened link into your Twitter compose box.

Step 4: Copy the newly shortened link.

USING IMAGES IN TWEETS

Twitter now enables users to upload photos and images to their tweets. This means that you can now share pictures with your followers by including them in your messages. However, there are some restrictions.

- **File size**: You can upload images up to 3 MB.

- **Format**: Twitter accepts GIF (non-animated), JPEG and PNG files.

- **Image size**: Twitter will scale your picture automatically so it fits in your tweet and Twitter feed.

- **Number**: You can only upload one image per tweet.

Hot Tip

If you upload a large or oddly shaped image, Twitter will scale or hide it in a user's timeline, but, by clicking Expand or Show image, a user can see the full picture.

How to Use Images

You can attach an image to any tweet, even protected ones. Images may appear in Twitter searches, but those attached to protected tweets won't. If you wish to remove an image from Twitter, you have to delete the tweet containing it. Each uploaded picture is assigned a shortened URL, which will reduce the character count available in your tweet. You can send images in both tweets and direct messages.

Left: Add images to your tweets to make them more eye-catching.

UPLOADING IMAGES TO TWEETS

1. In order to upload an image into a tweet, simply click the camera icon underneath the compose box.

2. Select the image you want to upload from your computer and click Open. You will then see a thumbnail of your picture beneath the compose box.

3. Compose the rest of your tweet and send.

4. You can remove an image before you send your message by clicking the X on the thumbnail.

Step 1: Click the camera icon.

Step 3: Add the text for your tweet.

Step 2: Click Share.

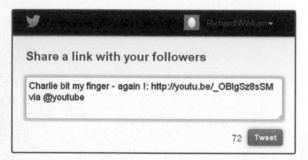

Step 3: A new window will open with the name and URL of the video.

Step 4: Click 'Tweet'. The video will now appear in your Twitter feed.

VIDEOS

Unfortunately, at the time of writing this book, Twitter does not offer the facility to upload videos into tweets. However, YouTube does allow you to embed videos in your messages.

1.   Sign in to Twitter, then visit YouTube and find the video you want to tweet.

2.   Click the link below the video that says Share.

3.   A box will appear; click the Twitter icon. A new window will open with a tweet box, along with the name of the video and its URL.

4.   Add your message to the video and click the Tweet button.

Hot Tip

If you are using a smartphone, you have the option to take a photo when you click the camera icon on Twitter.

TWITTIQUETTE

All sorts of conventions and unwritten rules have developed around using Twitter; therefore, not knowing what you should and should not do can be an obstacle in gaining followers and getting retweets.

UNSPOKEN RULES

Twitter can be a quagmire of social conventions and, for somebody who is new to the social media platform, it is all too easy to break many of the unspoken rules for acceptable behaviour on Twitter.

POSTING

What you say, how you say it and how often you post can be determining factors in how attractive you are to potential followers. Ensuring that you are setting the right tone and are posting the right content is the first step towards avoiding a Twitter faux pas. The tone of your tweets can also affect how often your messages are retweeted and favorited.

- **Content:** Even if you only intend your followers to see something, there is a possibility that your message will spread, so never say anything you would not want the whole world to see.

- **Too much information:** The minutiae of your life probably will not appeal to other people – and definitely never tweet about anything that happens in the bedroom or bathroom.

- **Spoilers:** No matter how great the film you saw last night was, do not give away the ending. People hate spoilers, and nothing will upset your Twitter followers more than you ruining a book, film or TV show for them.

- **Self-opinionated:** Not everybody will share the same views as you, so avoid getting on your soapbox, especially when it comes to politics or religion.

Frequency
Another way your content can lose followers is if there is too much of it. Try not to bombard your followers with tweets every few minutes. Tweet when you have something to say. However, not tweeting very often can have a similar effect, so try to find a happy medium.

Above: It is bad Twitter etiquette to follow someone just so they will follow you, then unfollow them again.

FOLLOWING
Just because somebody has followed you doesn't mean that you have to reciprocate. Following people for the sake of it will make you look like a spambot or somebody with no focus. Only follow those who share your interests. Don't forget that Twitter limits the number of people you can follow, so don't waste your time on people you have no interest in hearing from. However, if you know somebody personally, perhaps a colleague or friend, not following them back may make the next time you see them a little awkward.

Being Followed

Just as you are under no obligation to follow people, neither are others. Do not get angry when somebody does not follow you back. In addition, if somebody unfollows you, don't take it personally and certainly don't denounce them publicly.

Hot Tip

One of the biggest cardinal sins on Twitter is following somebody so that they will follow you back and then unfollowing them shortly after.

INTERACTIONS

Twitter is all about interaction. However, a lot of people sign up to Twitter and just read what others have written, rarely sending tweets or conversing with other users. This is fine, if that is what you want from Twitter. However, you cannot expect to build up followers that way, so you will need to engage with other users.

Mentioning People

You do not need to be shy about mentioning people, even if somebody is a household name or celebrity. Do not be afraid to ask

Hot Tip

If you are saying something negative about somebody on Twitter, do not use their Twitter handle (with the @ symbol), as this will ensure that they will see the message, which is the same as saying it to their face.

Above: Interact with other users by mentioning them in your tweets.

them a question or send them a tweet. However, do not expect a reply every time. Some people receive thousands of mentions a day and therefore cannot possibly reply to them all.

Direct Messages

If somebody sends you a direct message, do not respond publicly, as there is a chance that that person wants the conversation to remain private. In addition, if you receive a direct message, it is considered more of a slight if you do not reply compared to when you fail to reply to a regular tweet.

Retweets

If you see something witty or insightful on Twitter, never cut and paste the tweet and try to pass it off as your own – retweet the message instead. If you wish to add a comment, paste the tweet in, but make sure that you cite the original tweeter by including the abbreviation RT along with their Twitter handle.

PROMOTION

Twitter is a great tool for promotion, and many users expect a certain level of it. However, if you only tweet links to your work, website or blog, people will soon tire of you. If you do not want to lose followers, make sure that you are tweeting useful information, engaging with other users and sharing content, as well as sending out promotional messages.

AUTOMATED TWEETS

People hate spam and can detest automated messages. While many Twitter platforms enable you to send automated tweets, avoid doing it too often. Even an automated 'thanks for the follow' may be considered bad form. Only use automation when absolutely necessary, and it is often a good idea to let users know when a tweet is automated.

SOME OTHER TWITTER ETIQUETTE TIPS

As is the case with other social interactions, general good manners are expected on Twitter.

- **Thanking people:** If people follow or retweet you, thank them. It will go a long way to build up Twitter friendships.

- **Politeness:** Always be polite to people, no matter how much you disagree with them. Rudeness is one of the quickest ways to get blocked or unfollowed.

- **Offensive tweets:** Never post anything that may cause offence, even if done in good humour.

- **Apologizing:** If you upset somebody on Twitter or cause offence, an apology can go a long way in putting things right, so do not be afraid to say sorry.

FRIENDS AND FOLLOWERS

HOW TO FOLLOW

Twitter is all about following people, which allows you to see what other people are saying. However, it can be tricky at first to know who to follow and how to find them among such a vast number of Twitter users.

FOLLOWING

In order to see what other people are saying, you need to follow them. Additionally, following people means that you can interact with them in several ways.

- **Twitter feed:** The tweets of people you follow appear in your Twitter feed.

- **Updates:** Whenever somebody you follow 'favorites' a tweet, follows somebody else or sends a retweet, you can see it in the Activity section of your # Discover page.

- **Direct messages:** When you follow somebody, you will be able to receive direct messages from them.

- **Visibility:** Other people will be able to see the people you are following in both your profile and the profiles of the people you are following.

- **Notification:** Twitter will notify a person when you start following them.

Left: You can look at lists of your Twitter followers and check whether you are following them back.

The Follow Button

Following somebody is incredibly easy:

1. Click on the name of the person you want to follow.

2. When their profile summary pops up, simply click the Follow button.

Top Twitter Accounts

When you first join Twitter and begin tweeting, you may only get one or two followers. This is normal, as it does take time to build up a list of followers – unless you are a household name, of course. Many celebrities and public figures have millions of followers. Here are the top Twitter accounts as of mid 2014.

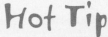

Step 2: To start following somebody new, simply click on their name and click the Follow button.

Hot Tip

If you are already following somebody, the Follow button will be blue and will say Following.

- **Katy Perry**: The pop singer has over 51 million followers.

- **Justin Bieber**: Close behind Katy Perry is Justin Bieber, who has nearly 50 million followers.

- **Barack Obama**: The US President is the third most popular person on Twitter, with over 41 million followers.

Above: Barack Obama has over 41 million followers on Twitter – and counting.

- **Lady Gaga**: With 41 million followers, Lady Gaga is the fourth most popular person.

FINDING PEOPLE TO FOLLOW

One of the most daunting aspects of Twitter for beginners is working out who to follow. The Twitterverse is vast, with millions of users online, and you cannot follow them all, so how do you find people with similar interests or even those you already know?

Above: The simplest way to search for people to follow on Twitter is to type their name in the search box.

Name Searches

The simplest way to find people on Twitter is to look for their name in the search box. If you know somebody's Twitter handle, you can search for it using the @ symbol; otherwise, you can also search for people by their real names. When you start typing, Twitter will give you suggestions based on the most popular people.

Finding Friends and Contacts

One useful function that Twitter provides for its users is the ability to search through email contacts to find existing friends and family members who may be on the platform. In order for Twitter to find people you know, you will have to allow access to your email accounts, which you can grant in the Find friends menu on the # Discover page (for more information on granting email access, *see* page 59).

TWITTER SUGGESTIONS

Twitter does suggest people you may want to consider following; this is based on who you are currently following, who those people are following, common subjects you tweet about and the most popular accounts on Twitter.

This is what you need to do in order to view Twitter's suggestions:

1. Go to the # Discover page and click on Who to follow.

2. Scroll down the list of suggestions.

3. Click Follow when you come across any user who you find interesting.

DISCOVERING NEW PEOPLE

Once you have found your existing friends and contacts on Twitter, and have browsed through Twitter suggestions, you may want to look for other people to follow.

Step 1: Visit the Who to follow page to discover suggestions for new people you could start following.

Following Followers

One of the simplest ways of finding people to follow is by searching through the followers of people you are already following. This is often a good way of finding like-minded individuals with similar interests. In order to do this, simply click on the person's name in your

Right: Searching through a follower's followers is a good way to find individuals with similar interests.

Twitter feed and then select Followers to bring up a list of all the people who are following them.

HOW MANY PEOPLE TO FOLLOW

Twitter monitors people who follow other users aggressively in a bid to then be followed. In addition, it monitors those people who follow and then quickly unfollow afterwards. In order to prevent this kind of aggressive following, Twitter imposes certain restrictions or limits, which apply after an individual has followed more than 2,000 users. Follow limits are different for each account and are based on the user's ratio of followers to following.

Above: Check your homepage to see how many people you are following, and click to see who they are.

Following Statistics

You can keep track of the number of people you are following on your homepage. Just above the compose box, you will see the number of people you are following, as well as how many people are following you. Simply click this number to view a list of all the people.

Protected Accounts

Not all users can be followed by simply clicking the Follow button, as some people have protected their tweets (for more information on this, *see* Chapter Two). You can only follow these people with their approval. This means that when you click Follow, that person will be notified of your request and will approve or decline it.

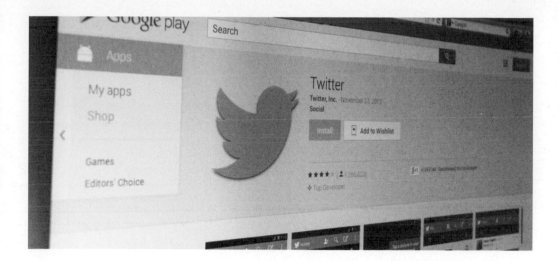

Accounts to Avoid

There are certain accounts on Twitter that it is best to avoid:

○ **Spammers**: Because of its reach, spammers use Twitter for aggressive marketing practices. Make sure that you read the sort of content people are tweeting about before you follow them.

Hot Tip

Before you follow someone, have a look at his or her activity and recent tweets. Anybody who sends more than 100 messages a day is either going to be a spammer or has far too much time on their hands to have anything of interest to say.

Above: A warning tweet from a user who thinks his account has been hijacked and is sending out spam.

- **Fraudsters**: Beware of people who just tweet links without any accompanying text, or those who suggest that there is a photograph or article about somebody on an external website.

- **Loquacious twitterers**: While harmless enough, some people are addicted to Twitter and tweet far too much, filling your Twitter feed with boring observations and comments.

UNFOLLOWING

If some of the people you follow are not providing any useful content for you, you can stop following their accounts at any time. This will remove those people's tweets from your Twitter feed. While Twitter notifies a user when you follow them, it does not let people know when you unfollow them, so do not be afraid of negative reactions.

Step 3: You can unfollow an account at any time if you are not finding their tweets useful or interesting.

1. Go into the list of people you are following and find the account you want to unfollow.

2. Hover the mouse over the Following button. It should change to red and say Unfollow.

3. Click to unfollow. Alternatively, you can click the Unfollow button on a user's profile page.

FOLLOWING TOOLS

While Twitter does provide you with many tools to find followers and monitor the activity of those you are following, there are services you can use to make these tasks much easier.

Justunfollow.com

This convenient service lets you know when any follower unfollows you; it also tells you who recently followed you, monitors the activity of people you follow, such as how often they tweet, and places people on a white or black list.

Above: TwitterLocal.com is a useful service for meeting new people locally who are on Twitter.

Twitterlocal.net

This is a great tool for finding who is on Twitter in your area. TwitterLocal lets you search for people who live within 40 miles of your home, thus making it a useful tool if you are using Twitter to meet new people locally.

Twitterpacks.pbworks.com

TwitterPacks lets you arrange Twitter users into groups based on interests and favourite topics, which makes it a really useful service for finding like-minded people.

BEING FOLLOWED

As there is little point in tweeting if nobody sees what you say, gaining followers is the goal for most Twitter users. The more people who follow you, the larger your audience, but getting followers is no easy task.

YOUR FOLLOWERS

Just as you can follow people on Twitter to see their tweets in your Twitter feed, people can follow you and see what you tweet about.

Tracking Your Followers

You can see how many people are following you on your homepage. The number of followers you have is listed next to how many people you are following, above the compose box. Your profile page also shows how many followers you have, and this information is available to anybody who clicks on your profile.

Notifications

By default, Twitter will send you an email every time you have a new follower. However, you can turn off this notification if you so wish (*see* Chapter Five for more information on notifications).

Left: You can check how many people are following you by visiting your profile page.

BUILDING UP A FOLLOWING

By far the hardest aspect of being on Twitter is building up a following. Your followers are your audience, so the more people you have following you, the more people will read your tweets. Some individuals employ all sorts of tactics to get others to follow them, but there is no easy way of building up a following other than ensuring that you are engaging positively with the Twitter community and sending out regular tweets.

Writing Quality Tweets

Just as with any form of blogging, by far the best way of building up a platform on Twitter is to make sure that you are putting out content that people will want to read. The higher the quality of your tweets, the more likely it will be that they are going to be retweeted, thus helping you to attract more followers.

Above: The best way to build a following on Twitter is to engage with the community by sending out regular tweets.

ENGAGING WITH OTHERS

One of the simplest ways of engaging with the Twitter community is to follow other people. Quite often, when you follow people, they will follow you back. However, unless you are putting out good-quality information, it is likely that they will eventually unfollow you.

Replies, Mentions and Retweets

Another way of engaging with the Twitter community is to reply directly to what people have tweeted, and add your own comments and opinions to what they have said. You can also mention people and retweet some of their content. If you interact and engage with people, they will be more likely to want to follow you.

Follower Number

Some people only follow individuals who have a certain number of followers. This can of course be a Catch 22 situation: how do you get followers if people will not follow you? For this reason, many people find that their follow numbers build up slowly until they reach a certain level and then increase dramatically.

Above: If you have only a small number of followers on Twitter, new followers may be put off.

WHY AREN'T PEOPLE FOLLOWING ME?

Despite engaging positively with the Twitter community, some people find that they still cannot build up much of a following. Often, this is because there is something putting people off.

Profile

Your profile can make a big difference when it comes to whether somebody will follow you or not.

Above: Your Twitter profile is an important tool – it can make the difference between putting off and attracting new followers.

○ **Biography:** Make sure that you explain who you are and what interests you. Try to avoid making overt political, religious or controversial statements, as this will certainly put some people off.

○ **Photo:** People like to put a face to a name; therefore, having the default egg image instead of a profile picture will certainly discourage people from wanting to follow you.

Hot Tip

Potential followers may be put off if you tweet too often, as they may not want their Twitter feed filled up. On the other hand, if you hardly ever tweet, then people may think that you are not worth following.

BLOCKING FOLLOWERS

If you do not want to be followed by somebody, or want to stop an existing follower from following you, you can block their account. Once blocked, a user will no longer be able to do certain things.

○ **Follow you:** They will no longer see your tweets in their Twitter feed.

○ **Lists:** A blocked user cannot add you to any lists.

○ **Reply or mention:** While they can still mention you in a tweet, you will no longer see it on your Mentions page.

Please note that unless you protect your tweets, they will still be available for anybody to see on your profile page, even non-account holders – and even if you have blocked a user.

Step 4: Select the 'Block' option in the scroll-down menu to prevent somebody from following you.

Blocking a User

This is what you need to do in order to block somebody from following you:

1. Click the Twitter handle of the person you want to block.

2. Click the Settings icon (gear wheel). next to the Following button.

3. Select 'Block @*username*' from the drop-down menu.

4. You can unblock a user by selecting Unblock from the same menu.

Reporting Followers

Sometimes, people post content on Twitter that you may think is inappropriate. Twitter has a facility for you to report all sorts of content. You can report any user for sending spam or pornographic images by clicking the Settings icon in their profile and using the report function in the drop-down menu. For other violations of Twitter's terms of service, fill in the appropriate form at https://support.twitter.com/forms.

Approving Followers

If you do not want just anybody following you, you can choose to protect your tweets. This means that you will have to approve any requests to follow you. However, you may find that few people will want to follow you if your messages are protected (for more information on how to protect your tweets, see page 89).

Above: If somebody you follow is posting inappropriate content, you can report them for spam.

Hot Tip

Avoid third-party applications that promise to get you followers. These are against Twitter's terms of service and can result in your account being suspended.

DIRECT MESSAGING

Twitter is a public forum where anybody can see what you are saying. However, you can also send direct messages, which will enable you to speak to people privately.

DMS

Direct messages, often called DMs, allow you to tweet privately to an individual on Twitter. Thanks to DMs, you can send and receive tweets without anybody else seeing the content, but there are restrictions to using them:

- **Who**: You can only send a DM to somebody following you and you can only receive a DM from somebody you follow.

- **Individual**: You cannot send a DM to more than one person at a time. If you wish to send a private message to multiple individuals, you have to send them separately.

Above: Sending a DM allows you to send a private tweet to an individual on Twitter.

> ## Hot Tip
>
> Twitter often changes the way it does things, and some people can now send and receive DMs to more than just their followers – a feature that may be rolled out to all users in the future.

○ **Tweet length**: DMs are the same as tweets. In other words, your message has to be contained within 140 characters.

HOW TO SEND A DM

Sending a direct message is relatively simple.

1. Click the envelope icon on the top right of your Twitter interface.

2. In the pop-up, click New message.

3. Type the name of the Twitter follower you want to message (remember the @ sign). Twitter may offer suggestions as you begin typing.

4. Compose your DM and click Send message.

Seeing DMs Sent to You

When you receive DMs, a blue number will appear in the corner of the envelope icon, indicating how many unread messages there are in your message box. In order to view your DMs, click the icon. You can also mark a DM as read by clicking the tick icon at the top of the pop-up screen.

Step 1: Click on the envelope icon to check for, or send, DMs.

Step 4: Once you have composed your DM, simply click the Send message button.

Above: The envelope icon will indicate when you have a new DM.

Responding to a DM

If you want to reply to a DM, click the message from the person you want to reply to, compose your message in the tweet box and click Send message. However, you cannot reply to a DM if that person is not following you.

Deleting a Direct Message

If you want to delete a direct message, click it in the DM pop-up window and then click the trash can icon. Please note that if you delete a DM, it disappears from both the sender's sent box and the recipient's inbox, so if a message has vanished, check with the sender, as they may have deleted it.

USING IMAGES AND LINKS IN DMS

Just as with regular tweets, you can send both links and images in direct messages. Of course, any image you send in a DM will only be visible to the person you have sent it to. In order to include an image in a DM, simply click the camera icon at the bottom of the DM pop-up screen. Links can be pasted in the normal way.

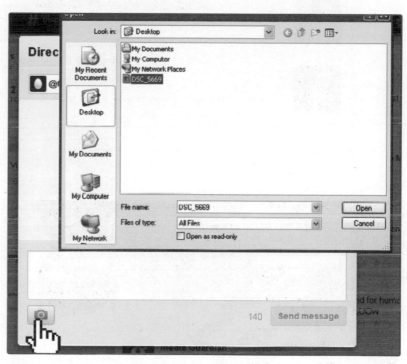

Above: You can add an image to a DM by clicking the camera icon and selecting the image you wish to insert.

PRIVACY AND SECURITY

A common problem with DMs is that malicious users are increasingly using them to send spam tweets. If you receive a DM from somebody you are following that looks like spam, it could be an indication that their account has been hacked. You can report the message as spam by clicking on the icon that looks like a no-entry sign in the DM pop-up window, but make sure that you tell the person whose account it is that you have done this.

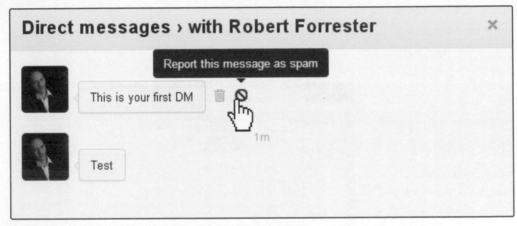

Above: If you receive a DM that looks like spam, you should report it by clicking the icon that looks like a no-entry sign.

DM Marketing

While not currently available on all accounts at the time of writing this book, Twitter is allowing some account holders to opt into a scheme that lets them receive DMs from all users. This is most likely going to provide an added marketing channel to businesses, enabling them to send DMs to customers with potential discounts and news on product releases. For those who do not want to receive such messages, Twitter will most likely provide the option to opt out.

NURTURING YOUR AUDIENCE

Getting followers on Twitter is one thing, but keeping them is another. Twitter users can be fickle and, unless you are providing interesting content and interacting positively with them, they may soon unfollow you. In order to hang on to them, you need to keep your followers engaged.

ENGAGING WITH FOLLOWERS

Failing to interact positively with people will soon have them unfollowing you, so you need to know how and when to engage with your followers – and that means nurturing your audience.

Follower Activity

Learn when your followers are active. Due to the sheer volume of content being tweeted every day, you cannot expect your followers to see your messages if you send them out when they are not online. Tweets have a time and date stamp on them to help you identify when users are active, so send out your tweets to suit this time.

Take the Lead

Do not wait for your followers to engage with you: be proactive. Ask your followers questions, reply to comments they make and retweet any interesting tweets that they may have sent.

Above: Each tweet has a time and date stamp, which indicates when users are active; send your tweets to suit this time.

Keep Conversations Going

When somebody replies to one of your tweets, keep the conversation going as much as possible. This is especially relevant for anybody using Twitter for promotion or business, as it keeps your name in circulation and shows positive interactions. You can maintain this positive image and exchange by retweeting helpful comments and replies.

FOLLOWERS AND FOLLOWING

When people look at a profile to decide whether somebody is worth following, it is common for them to look at the followers-to-following ratio. Try to maintain a higher level of followers than the people you are following. This will suggest that you are a compelling Twitter user and in demand. Therefore, when you follow somebody, they may feel a sense of privilege and are less likely to unfollow you.

Hot Tip

If your Twitter followers have a blog, tweeting links to their posts is a sure-fire way of getting retweets.

44,751
TWEETS
1,069
FOLLOWING
1,791,587
FOLLOWERS
Follow
Followed by Jonathan Rashad, Press Gazette and Journalism.co.uk.
The Guardian @guardian
3m
Ali Larayedh resigns as Tunisia's PM to make way for caretaker government: gu.com/p/3yyyc/tf
Details
The Guardian @guardian
4m
Met police hope personal cameras can restore trust after Mark Duggan killing

Above: Try to keep a higher number of followers than the number of people you are following, as this will attract more followers.

Following Maintenance

Every now and again, you may want to go through the list of users who you are following and make changes. If people are rarely tweeting or you have had few interactions with them, it may be worth unfollowing them to make room for those with whom you may have more contact.

Be Picky

When you start building up a list of followers, don't just follow anybody who follows you or who you find vaguely interesting; instead, only follow somebody if you think you will gain a positive interaction. Use their profile information to help you make a decision.

○ **Follower number:** If a user has only a few followers – or they are following more people than they have followers – then they may not be worth following.

Above: A user's profile, showing the number of tweets they have posted and their follower-to-following ratio.

- **Tweets**: How often does a person tweet? Only follow those people who actively engage regularly.

- **Followers**: Do you share followers with a user? This is a good indication that you may have something in common with them. Use Twitter suggestions to find like-minded people.

Hot Tip

Set yourself a minimum number of tweets every day. Do not overdo it though, and only tweet about things that you think your followers will be interested in.

Top Followers

After a while, you will start to develop closer Twitter relationships with a certain number of followers. As you will correspond with these people regularly, make sure that you nurture them. Treat them as you would friends in real life and interact with them frequently. Retweet and 'favorite' their tweets, and reply to their messages. Additionally, keep an eye on their activity and see who they are following and interacting with, in order to identify new people to follow.

Timely Responses

Although nobody should spend all day on Twitter, there is little point in sending a reply to a tweet or direct message hours or even days after it has been sent. Try to respond as soon as you can (*see* Chapter Five for various tools and apps that can alert you to mentions and tweets). In addition, take advantage of email notifications.

Left: The @ connect page shows you a timeline of all your Twitter interactions.

TWITTER AND BLOGGING

Twitter is the perfect way to complement a blog, as you can use it to build up a blog audience. However, if you don't have a blog but are regularly tweeting on certain subjects, you may find that a blog is a better outlet for your ideas.

TWITTER AS A BLOGGING PLATFORM

Twitter is essentially a blogging platform. As with all blogs, you can express your ideas in a tweet and publish it for the world to see. However, Twitter does differ in several ways to a regular blog:

Above: The Twitter platform also has its own official blog (blog.twitter.com).

- **Microblog:** Your blog posts cannot exceed 140 characters, which is why Twitter is known as a microblog.

- **Audience:** Rather than people visiting your individual blog, Twitter has an existing audience of millions of individuals, making it much easier to reach people with your posts.

- **Followers:** If somebody wants to read your regular blog, they have to visit its URL. Twitter automatically feeds your posts to those following you.

- **Interaction:** While most blogs allow comments, Twitter can provide instantaneous replies, mentions and retweets to the things that you write.

Microblogging

The main problem faced by many users of Twitter is space, as 140 characters is not a lot of room to express your ideas. Some people find that they end up sending dozens of tweets on the same subject one after another; therefore, it would be far simpler for them to maintain a blog and use Twitter to bring an audience to it.

HAND IN HAND

Whether you have an existing blog that you want to promote, or you want to start a blog and take advantage of the following that you have built up on Twitter, blogging and Twitter go hand in hand.

Complementing Your Blog

No other platform is better at promoting your blog than Twitter.

○ **Audience**: Twitter makes it easy to find people interested in the subject of your blog. If someone is following you because they like what you say, then they may be interested in your blog too.

○ **Links**: You can use Twitter to send links to your blog. A tweet is the perfect size to contain your next blog post's title and a link.

○ **Sharing**: Twitter makes it easy for others to share links to your blog posts.

Above: You can use Twitter to promote your blog by tweeting links to new blog posts.

INTEGRATING TWITTER WITH YOUR BLOG

In order to promote your blog using Twitter, you need to ensure that it is as Twitter-friendly as possible. You can do this by adding various features to your blog to make it easy for users to follow, share and interact with it.

Share Buttons

Most blogging platforms now incorporate social media buttons at the bottom of posts. Make sure that these are switched on, as users can share your blog posts with their Twitter followers by simply clicking the button. This will help you to build up a larger audience for your blog.

I believe that's the kind of agent that authors need. Not the kind worrie

If you'd like to respond, Mr. Gernert, you can do so in the comments an email me directly. I won't edit anything you write, and I'm happy to pro questions and maybe clarify your point of view.

POSTED BY JOE KONRATH AT 6:29 PM   75 COMMENTS:

M B t f g+1 +18 Recommend this on Google

Above: Including sharing buttons on your blog means that both you and your readers can share a post on Twitter.

Follow Buttons

While you may want to use Twitter to build up your blog audience, you can also attract followers from your blog. The best way to do this is to include a 'Follow Me' button somewhere on your blog. When clicked, this automatically takes a user to their Twitter account, where they can see your profile and follow you.

Hot Tip

You can download widgets or follow buttons for most blogging platforms for inclusion in your blog.

Step 2: Once you have clicked 'More', simply select the 'Embed Tweet' option.

Step 3: To finish the embedding, copy the code and paste it into your blog, making sure to use HTML mode.

Embedding Tweets

Twitter provides a useful function for bloggers that lets them include tweets in their blog posts. This is known as embedding tweets and it is incredibly simple to do:

1.   Find the tweet that you want to embed in your blog and click the 'More' link on the bottom right.

2.   Click 'Embed Tweet'. A pop-up window will appear, containing a long line of code.

3.   Copy the code and paste it into your blog. Make sure that you use HTML mode when pasting.

4.   The tweet should now appear in your blog post.

TWITTER FEEDS

For real interaction with Twitter, you can include a feed from your blog to your Twitter account, allowing your followers to see your latest posts as and when you add them. However, setting up a Twitter feed can be a little complicated. Perhaps the easiest way to do this is to sign up to a free service such as twitterfeed.com. These services make including a Twitter feed much simpler, and also provide you with tracking and statistics.

Step 1: You can sign into Twitterfeed.com using existing mail or other accounts.

Setting up a Feed Using Twitterfeed

A service such as Twitterfeed can be used on most blogging and web platforms.

1. Sign into twitterfeed.com using one of the listed blogging platforms and email accounts, such as WordPress, Blogger or Gmail.

2. Enter the URL to your blog or website.

3. Click 'Continue to Step 2'.

4. Click on the Twitter link and click the 'Authenticate Twitter' button.

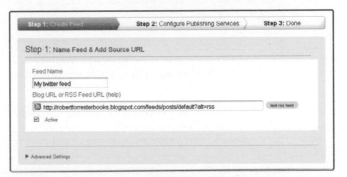

Step 2: Add your blog details by entering the URL to your blog or website.

Step 4: You will need to authenticate your Twitter feed by clicking the 'Authenticate Twitter' button.

5.   You will be taken to Twitter, where you have to confirm that you want to 'Authorize the app'. Click the button.

6.   Click 'Create Service'. Every time you create a blog post, the title and link will now appear on Twitter.

Twitter Feed on Your Blog

You can also include a feed from your Twitter account on your blog. When you install these feeds, all your latest blog posts appear in a window in your Twitter feed. This can help to attract followers from people reading your blog posts.

1.   Log into Twitter, go to Settings (gear wheel icon menu) and select Widgets.

2.   Click 'Create new' and choose the type of feed, such as user timeline, favorites or lists.

3.   Customize the design of your feed by changing colours and size.

Step 2: To include a feed from your Twitter account on your blog, you will need to begin by creating a new widget.

4. Click 'Create widget'.
You will see a box
containing some HTML
code. Simply copy this
code and use it on your
website or blog. Most web
and blogging software will
have an option to view
and edit a page's HTML.
You should use this mode
when pasting in your
Twitter feed code.

Step 4: To finish embedding a Twitter feed into your blog, copy the HTML code and paste it into your blog.

TWITTER TIPS
FOR BLOGGERS

If you are using Twitter to promote your blog,
you may find the following tips useful.

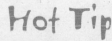

Hot Tip

For more useful tools for
integrating your blog with
Twitter, see the widgets
section on page 181.

○ **Links**: Do not just link to your blog posts; also tweet
comments and other interactions from blog readers.

○ **Do not over-promote**: Make sure that you are not just using Twitter to advertise your
blog. Mix your promotional tweets with other interactions.

○ **Subscribers**: Make sure that you follow your blog subscribers on Twitter and interact with
them. Use Twitter to connect to your blog's audience.

○ **Audience**: Use Twitter to find like-minded people who may be interested in your blog.
Follow them and send them links to content you think they may be interested in.

EVERYDAY TWITTER

MAKING THE MOST OF TWITTER

Beyond the basic elements, Twitter has many useful features that can help you to maximize your experience. In this chapter, we will discuss some of the best ways to utilize Twitter, as well as how to handle some of the negative aspects of using social media.

USING TWITTER

Once you start getting to grips with Twitter, and are tweeting, replying and mentioning others in your tweets, you will find that there are additional useful features that you can use to engage with other users. Using Twitter can go beyond just regular tweeting and replying, and you will find many different ways of socializing, promoting or finding useful information.

Above: You can add tweets to your 'Favorites' folder so that you can refer to it later.

FAVORITE TWEETS

Sometimes, you might come across a tweet that you want to read later. Twitter provides you the facility to 'favorite' a tweet, which places it in your 'Favorites' folder, located on the Me page on your Twitter interface. The person who wrote the tweet can see who has favorited it on their @ Connect page. There are several reasons why people favorite tweets:

Above: Favorited tweets will show up on the @ Connect page, and this can help you to get noticed by the person who posted it.

Hot Tip

If somebody tweets something that you enjoyed, but you do not think it is suitable to retweet to your followers, favorite it to show your appreciation to the original poster.

○ **Save for later:** If a tweet has a useful link that you do not have time to visit there and then, you can favorite it so that you can find it again easily later.

○ **Showing appreciation:** When you favorite a tweet, it lets the user know that you liked what they tweeted.

Step 2: It is easy to favorite a tweet; simply click the Favorite button.

○ **Draw a user's attention:** Favoriting somebody's tweet can help to get you noticed by the person who posted it, who may decide to follow you.

How to Favorite a Tweet

1. Hover your mouse over the tweet you want to favorite.

2. Click Favorite. A yellow-bordered star should appear in the right-hand corner of the tweet.

3. You can un-favorite a tweet by clicking the Favorite button again, and you will see the yellow-bordered star disappears. This will remove the tweet from your Favorites list.

TOPIC SEARCHING

With over 200 million users constantly tweeting about everything and anything, Twitter contains a wealth of useful information. However, with so much traffic, gaining access to what you want is not easy. Thankfully, Twitter's search function is a useful tool for finding the information you need, and you can use it in several ways:

Above: To search for tweets relating to a particular topic, try making a hashtag search.

> ### Hot Tip
> Twitter has its own search engine page – https://search.twitter.com – which you can use just like Google for finding topics on Twitter.

- **People:** Use the @ symbol to find Twitter handles or simply type in a person's name.

- **Keywords:** Enter the keywords to obtain a list of tweets containing that topic.

- **Hashtags:** A more direct and easier way to gain the information you want.

Making Searches on Twitter

Twitter's search engine has some useful features to help you find the information you want.

- **Suggestions:** When you start typing, Twitter will make suggestions based on the most popular topic searches.

◦ **Fluid searching**: As people are constantly tweeting, when new results come in, Twitter will alert you to the new tweets at the top of the search results page.

Search Limitations

The biggest problem with making Twitter searches is the sheer volume of tweets in the archive. Since it is impossible to list everything, you may find that most searches are limited to just the last few days or weeks.

Advanced Searching

For a more specific search, you can use Twitter's advanced search feature, located at https://twitter.com/search-advanced, which allows you to be more specific with what you are looking for. For example, you will be able to include and exclude certain keywords

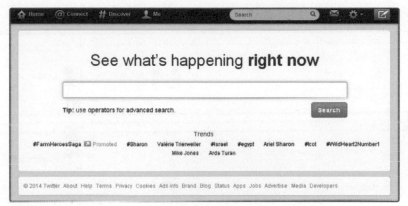

Above: Twitter's search page is a good way to find information; useful features include listing popular topic searches.

and hashtags or specify people and locations for Twitter to search (for more details on how to carry out advanced searches, *see* Chapter Seven).

TRENDING

Another great tool for finding information – particularly things that are currently happening in the news – is Twitter's trending topics. Trends, which can be seen on the left-hand side of your Twitter feed, are the most commonly tweeted-about subjects at any given time. They are based on both keywords and hashtags, and are often a great way to determine what is going on in the world.

Tracking Topics and Trends

You can take advantage of various third-party services that can help you to track certain topics and trends. These are particularly useful if you are using Twitter for research or business promotion, as they allow you to receive the very latest news and discussions on certain topics. We will go into more detail about third-party apps and services later in this chapter (*see page* 170), but here are some of the most useful ones for tracking trends and topics:

Above: You can see which topics are currently trending on Twitter by looking at the 'Trends' section on the homepage.

- **hashtags.org:** A website that shows you the most popular hashtags.

- **HootSuite:** Lets you track topics and receive the latest tweets containing certain keywords.

- **twitter.com/Trendrr:** Allows you to track trends and keywords.

EXPANDED TWEETS

Although tweets are meant to be just 140 characters, Twitter now includes an expanded tweet system, whereby if you tweet a link to a certain web page from one of Twitter's partner sites, Twitter will automatically summarize a version of the web page beneath the tweet. This allows you to see content previews and images, and even to play videos. Some of the partner sites you can link to include the following:

- **Dailymotion:** When you link to a video on Dailymotion, a Twitter user can expand the tweet and watch the video.

- **Amazon**: If you send a book link, Twitter users can expand it to see the cover and summary.

- **Time**: Post a link to an article on *Time* magazine and Twitter users will see a preview of the page.

- **Newspapers**: Expanded tweets also include links to news stories in the *Wall Street Journal* and other popular online newspapers.

Expanding a Tweet

1. An expanded tweet will contain a link saying: View summary or, in the case of a video, View media.

2. Click the link to expand the tweet.

3. Click Hide summary/Hide media to shrink the tweet again.

Above: Click 'Hide summary' to shrink an expanded tweet back to normal size.

Above: To view details of a tweet, such as time and date, click the 'Expand' link.

Hot Tip

Expanded tweets should not be confused with the Expand link on the bottom of most tweets, which is a feature that lets you see more details about the message.

TWEET DETAILS

Your Twitter feed contains the most essential elements of tweets, namely the content. However, you can see other details, such as the time and date when the tweet was sent, if you click the link that says Expand. If a tweet is a retweet, this feature also shows the number of retweets and favorites that the person who originally posted the message has, and pictures of some of their followers you may wish to follow.

Following Discussions

Often, you may come across a reply to a tweet and be interested in following the discussion; thankfully, Twitter makes it easy for you to follow conversations. If a tweet is a reply, it will contain a 'View conversation' link which, when clicked, will show the tweets in that conversation. These may include messages from a number of different people engaged in the discussion.

Above: Clicking 'View conversation' enables you to see if a tweet is a reply, and shows you all posts in the discussion.

Tweet Chats

Thanks to the ability to interact with large numbers of people in real time, Twitter is a great place to hold discussions, forums and Q&A sessions. Tweet chats are usually arranged in advance at a specific time,

Hot Tip

If you host a tweet chat, come up with a hashtag that users can include to filter all tweets into one conversation and which will make it easier for people to get involved.

when a Twitter user will host a conversation enabling those interested to ask questions and discuss certain topics.

Tweet Permalink Page

All tweets have their own webpage, as do conversation streams. If you click 'Expand' or 'View conversation', you should see a 'Details' link next to the time and date when the tweet was sent. If you click this link, you will be taken to the tweet's unique page, where the message will appear much larger and you will be able to see all details and replies to it.

Above: Each tweet has its own page where the post is enlarged and you can view details and replies.

Sharing Tweets

Tweets are very easy to share; you can send links to them by copying and pasting the URL from any tweet permalink page. In addition, you can share a tweet by email.

1. Click the More link on the bottom right of the tweet you want to share.

2. Click 'Share via email'.

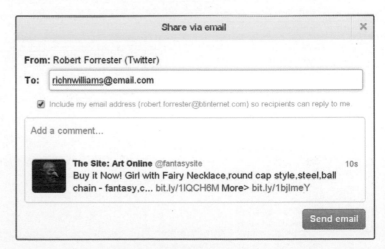

Step 2: To share a tweet by email, simply click 'Share via email' and enter the recipient's email address.

3. In the pop-up window, enter the email address of the person you want to send the tweet to.

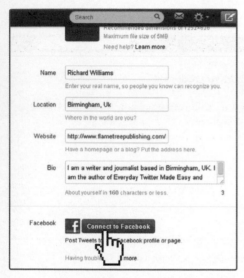

4. Add a comment if you wish and click the box to include or exclude your own email address.

5. Click 'Send email'.

INTEGRATING TWITTER WITH FACEBOOK

While Twitter is incredibly popular, Facebook is still the world's number one social media platform. Fortunately, it is easy to integrate your Twitter feed with your Facebook account. You can automatically post tweets to your Facebook wall or to your fan page, which means that all your Facebook friends and fans can see everything you tweet, even if they are not on Twitter.

Step 2: Connect your Twitter and Facebook accounts by clicking the 'Connect to Facebook' button.

Step 5: Select where on Facebook your tweets appear, such as your timeline or profile page.

Including a Twitter Feed on Facebook

1. Log into Twitter, click Settings (in the gear wheel menu) and then click Profile.

2. Scroll down and click Connect to Facebook and link your accounts

3. In the pop-up window, sign into Facebook.

4. Select where you want your tweets to appear, such as your timeline or profile page.

5. Click OK. Your tweets will now appear on Facebook, along with your Twitter handle.

INTEGRATING TWITTER WITH LINKEDIN

If you are using Twitter for business, you can also automatically tweet your LinkedIn status updates.

1. Log into LinkedIn and go into 'Account & Settings' (top right: the person icon).

2. Click 'Privacy & Settings'.

3. Click the 'Manage your Twitter settings' link.

4. Click 'Add your Twitter account', and enter your Twitter username and password or, if you are already logged in, click 'Authorize app'.

5. Click 'Save changes'.

EMAIL NOTIFICATIONS

In order to help you keep track of your interactions, Twitter can send you email notifications so that you do not miss that all-important tweet, reply, direct message or mention. You can receive an emall for all sorts of things.

Step 2: To tweet your LinkedIn status updates automatically, begin by selecting 'Privacy & Settings' from the 'Account & Settings' menu.

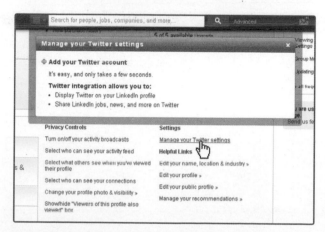

Step 4: Click 'Add your Twitter account', enter your details and authorize.

- **Favorites**: You can receive a notification when somebody favorites one of your tweets or a tweet that mentions you.

- **Mentions**: Twitter will email you if you are mentioned in a tweet.

- **Retweets**: Whenever one of your tweets is retweeted, Twitter can let you know.

Hot Tip

Twitter may also send you emails relating to their products and services, as well as offering you news updates. However, all notifications can be turned off.

- **Direct messages**: If somebody sends you a DM, you can read the message in your email rather than logging in.

- **Replies**: Email notifications let you know if somebody has replied to a tweet.

- **Followers**: If you have a new follower or somebody from your email address book joins Twitter, you can be notified.

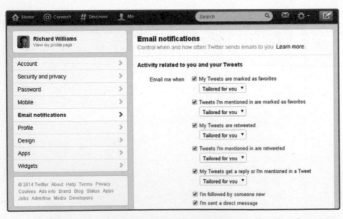

Step 2: To alter your email notifications settings, select 'Email notifications' from the Settings menu.

Turning Notifications On/Off

You can turn all notifications on or off, as well as receiving notifications tailored to you (from your followers) or relating to any interactions.

1. Go into the Settings menu (gear wheel icon on the top right).

2. Click on 'Email notifications' on the sidebar.

3. Check the relevant box to turn on a particular email notification and uncheck to turn it off. In the drop-down menu, choose whether to receive notifications from interactions from 'Anybody' or 'Tailored for you'.

4. Click Save changes to save your preferences.

TWITTER ADVERTS

Twitter is a free service, but as with all businesses, the company needs to make money. As is the case with other social media platforms, Twitter makes its money by selling advertising, which appears in various ways.

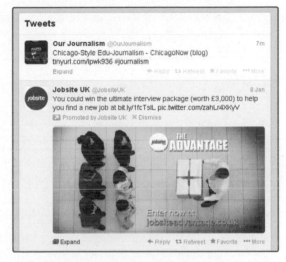

Promoted Tweets

Not all tweets in your Twitter feed will be from people you follow. Twitter also sends you messages that are paid for by advertisers. These promoted tweets are identifiable by an orange tick and the words 'Promoted by' followed by the Twitter handle of the advertiser.

Above: Promoted tweets are paid for by advertisers and can be identified by an icon and the words 'Promoted by'.

Dismissing Promoted Tweets

You cannot opt out of receiving promoted tweets, but you can remove them from your feed.

1. Hover your mouse over a particular promoted tweet.

2. A Dismiss link next to a cross will appear.

3. Click the link and the tweet will be removed from your Twitter feed.

Promoted Accounts

As well as promoted tweets, Twitter also offers advertisers the ability to become promoted accounts. These appear in your suggestions of people to follow and are identifiable by the orange tick and the word 'Promoted' beneath their profile. These promoted accounts are tailored specifically to different users, depending on the types of accounts that they normally follow.

Promoted Trends

Another form of advertising offered by Twitter is the promoted trend. Again, these are marked as promoted and appear at the top of Twitter's list of trends.

Political Adverts

Since Twitter has such a great reach and influence, it is an ideal platform for political advertisers. A purple 'Promoted' icon indicates when a tweet, account or trend is a political advertisement.

AUTOMATED TWEETS

Twitter is a platform for people, not robots, but many tweets you will come across are automated. Automation can be useful, but it is very easy to overdo it. In addition, Twitter has some guidelines about automated tweets regarding things you should and should not do:

Using Automation

Twitter accepts that it is fine to automate some things.

- **Feeds:** Twitter does not mind if you automate blog feeds or status updates from other social media platforms.

- **News and weather:** Automated tweets that provide useful information to Twitter users are also fine.

- **Updates:** If you have posted a video on YouTube or written a new blog post, it is OK to send an automated tweet about it.

Automated Account Actions

Twitter does not like it when you automate certain account actions:

- **Replies and mentions**: Do not automate replies and mentions, as this can get your account suspended.

- **Retweets**: Automated retweeting is also against Twitter's guidelines.

- **Following**: Accounts that use automation to follow and unfollow people may also be suspended.

Hot Tip

Many users use automation to thank others for following by direct message. While not against Twitter's guidelines, many users find this sort of automation annoying.

Spambots

Due to the ease of automation on Twitter, spambots (software that sends tweets) are a common problem. Often, these copy tweets from real people in a bid to appear human. If you think a spambot is sending you messages, you can report it by using the 'Report Tweet' link in the More drop-down menu at the bottom of the tweet.

NEGATIVE TWEETS

Twitter is generally a friendly place, but occasionally you will come across people who say unpleasant things. If somebody sends you a negative tweet, the simplest course of action is to unfollow that person. You can also block that user (*see pages 130–31* for more details). However, if you continue to receive replies, mentions or other interactions on Twitter that you consider abusive or constitute harassment, you can report their behaviour at https://support.twitter.com/forms/abusiveuser.

Above: If you repeatedly receive abusive interactions on Twitter, you can report the tweet, or even the user.

Trolls

Some people, often referred to as 'trolls', take pleasure in being abusive on social media platforms. While troll behaviour is often reported in the media, it is thankfully still quite rare. However, if you are receiving repeated abuse, or believe that you are being harassed or threatened in any way on Twitter, you should consider reporting the behaviour to the police, especially if a person is threatening violence towards you.

- **Twitter:** Make sure that you report the harassment to Twitter, which may be able to help in any future criminal investigation by revealing the IP address of the user in question.

- **Evidence:** Take screenshots or print-outs of any threatening messages.

- **Information:** Detail any information that may help the police to identify the user, such as if you have received unpleasant messages on other social media platforms.

Hot Tip

Many trolls and offensive Twitter users set up their accounts anonymously, for the purpose of sending abuse. Consider blocking anonymous users without a profile picture, especially those with only a few followers.

MOBILE TWITTER

The great thing about Twitter is that you do not need to be tied to your desktop computer to send and receive messages. The fact that you can literally tweet from anywhere using a mobile phone or tablet makes Twitter a truly versatile social media platform.

TWEETING ON YOUR PHONE

Twitter was the first social media platform that allowed interaction with mobile phones. Even before the days of smartphones and mobile internet, you could send tweets using the SMS feature on most mobiles. These days, most people use a Twitter app to send and receive tweets on the go, but Twitter still supports SMS tweeting.

Mobile Tweeting

Tweeting from your phone can add a new dimension to your messages. Going mobile means that you can tweet immediately, whenever something comes to mind, rather than having to wait until you are in front of a computer. This enables you to tweet from all sorts of places, from pop concerts and sporting events to sitting on a bus or train.

Tweeting on the Go

There are several ways to tweet whilst on a mobile device:

- **Mobile twitter**: Twitter has a mobile-friendly website – https://mobile.twitter.com – which provides a simpler interface than its normal web version.

- **Twitter apps**: You can download a Twitter app for most smartphone and tablet computer operating systems.

- **SMS**: You don't even need to own a smartphone or tablet to tweet on the go, as Twitter continues to support SMS texting.

Hot Tip

You cannot access the full Twitter website from a mobile, as Twitter will automatically recognize when you are using a mobile phone and will redirect you from twitter.com to mobile.twitter.com.

TWITTER MOBILE

The mobile version of Twitter (https://mobile.twitter.com) offers all the same features and usability as the full web version, but has been specifically designed to be more user friendly on a mobile phone or tablet. It also looks slightly different, as the interface is designed to fit on a smaller screen.

Using Twitter Mobile

Twitter mobile offers nearly all the same features as the full web version:

Above: The mobile Twitter interface is different to the full Twitter website, as it is designed for a smaller screen.

- **Sign up**: If you do not have a Twitter account, you can sign up on the mobile version.

- **Navigation**: mobile.twitter.com has a similar interface to the full site, with your @ Connect, # Discover and Me pages at the top of the homepage or down the side, depending on your device.

- **Tweeting**: You can send tweets and retweets just as easily from the mobile version as from the full website.

- **Twitter feed**: You can view all the latest tweets from people as and when they come in.

- **Replies, mentions and favorites**: You can reply to tweets, mention people and assign messages as favorites on the mobile version.

- **Following and follows**: As with the web version, you can follow people, see your followers' profiles and block users on the mobile version.

- **Direct messages**: You can also send and receive direct messages.

TWITTER MOBILE APPS

These days, most people who use Twitter on their mobile do so by using an app. Apps (applications) are simply programs that enable you to use Twitter without having to visit the mobile website. They often offer better mobile-friendly interaction, while providing all the same functionality as using Twitter on the web. Many people will find that a Twitter app is already installed on their mobile phone or tablet when they purchase it, but you can download the latest official apps from the app store associated with your device.

- **Android**: You can download the official Twitter app from the Google Play Store (https://play.google.com) for all Android devices.

- **iOS**: The App Store (https://itunes.apple.com) will have the latest Twitter app for iPhones and iPads.

- **Windows phones**: The latest Twitter app for Windows phones is available at the Windows Store (www.windowsphone.com).

- **Nokia**: The Nokia Store (http://store.ovi.com) has a Twitter app for Nokia users.

- **Blackberry**: You can install a Twitter app for both the BlackBerry 7 and BlackBerry 10 devices from BlackBerry World (http://appworld.blackberry.com).

Above: If you have an iOS device, you can download the Twitter app from iTunes.

Hot Tip

iOS and Android users can download the latest official Twitter app from the Twitter website: https://about.twitter.com/download.

Third-party Mobile Apps

If you do not like the official Twitter app for your device, you can download all sorts of third-party apps from the various app stores, which can help you manage your Twitter account on your mobile. Although these are not official Twitter applications, some do offer more functionality and better interfaces than the standard apps.

- **Tweetbot**: Only available for iOS, Tweetbot offers a simplified interface that makes tweeting on the iPhone incredibly user friendly (£2.99/$2.99 from the App Store).

- **HootSuite Mobile**: Available free for Android and iOS, HootSuite enables you not only to send and receive tweets, but also to schedule tweets, manage multiple users and even track analytics.

- **Echofon**: A free app for iOS and Android, Echofon offers photo previews as well as an intuitive interface that makes tweeting quick and simple.

- **Plume**: Only available for Android, this free app has many customization features and lets you manage multiple Twitter accounts.

Left: Echofon is a popular free mobile Twitter app which makes tweeting quick and simple.

SMS TWEETS

While most people access Twitter via an app or the mobile Twitter website, you can still send and receive tweets on your mobile phone using SMS. SMS interaction allows people without a smartphone or regular web access to use Twitter and is one of the reasons it has become such a powerful social media platform around the world, especially in places where the internet infrastructure is not as well developed as it is in the West.

Adding Your Phone to Twitter

In order to use Twitter's SMS integration, you first have to register your mobile number with your Twitter profile.

1. Log in to Twitter at twitter.com.

2. Click the Mobile link in the settings menu (click Settings in the gear icon drop-down menu).

3. Select your country/region and enter your phone number (the country code will already be included, so omit the initial zero).

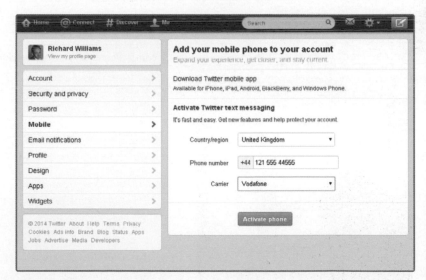

4. Choose your mobile operator where it says Carrier.

5. Click Activate phone.

Above: In order to use Twitter's SMS integration, you need to register your mobile number with your Twitter account.

6. Before you can begin using Twitter's SMS service, you have to verify your phone by sending 'GO' to your country's specific short code (*see* below).

Short Codes

A short code is a shorter phone number that allows two-way communication with Twitter. Most countries and carriers have Twitter short codes.

○ **UK**: The Twitter short code for most UK phone operators is 86444.

○ **USA**: The short code for all US phone operators is 40404.

○ **Other locations**: A full list of Twitter short codes is available on the platform's website at https://support.twitter.com/articles/20170024.

Sending SMS Tweets

Sending a tweet by SMS is simple:

1. Make sure that you have added your phone to your Twitter account and verified it.

2. Type your tweet in an SMS text box.

3. Send the SMS to your Twitter short code.

4. Your tweet will appear in your Twitter feed as normal.

Sending MMS Pictures

You can also attach images to your tweets by using a phone's MMS text message feature. Simply compose your

MMS text as normal, attach the image you want to tweet and send to your short code. Your image will appear below your message in people's Twitter feeds.

Receiving SMS Tweets

You can also receive tweets by SMS. However, rather than you being inundated with thousands of tweets from all the people you follow, you have to enable mobile notifications from specific people.

1. In the Settings menu, click the Mobile tab.

2. Where it says 'Text notifications', tick the box for 'Tweets from people you've enabled for mobile notifications'.

3. Visit the profile page of the Twitter user from whom you want to receive tweets by SMS and click the icon next to the Following button.

4. In the drop-down menu, select 'Turn on mobile notifications'.

SMS Notifications

You can also receive SMS notifications when you get replies, mentions or direct messages. In order to activate this, simply check the relevant boxes in the 'Text notifications' box in the Mobile settings menu. You can stop all tweets and notifications from being sent to your phone by texting OFF to your short code.

Hot Tip

Remember that although Twitter does not charge you for sending and receiving SMS tweets, your mobile operator may do so, depending on your call plan.

Step 4: Select 'Turn on mobile notifications' to receive tweets by SMS from specific people.

TWITTER CLIENTS, SERVICES AND WIDGETS

While twitter.com offers plenty of features and functionality, there are some things you cannot do using the Twitter website. Fortunately, there are plenty of Twitter clients, third-party services and widgets that can help you to get the most out of Twitter.

TWITTER CLIENTS

Twitter clients are software programs that run on your PC, Mac or phone and help you to manage your Twitter account. Many of these clients let you do things that you cannot do using the regular Twitter website or official apps.

- **Topic tracking**: Lets you track certain topics and hashtags, keeping you abreast of the latest news and information.

- **Scheduling tweets**: You can schedule tweets to appear at certain times.

- **Following management**: You can group your followers and see who unfollowed you, as well as who are the most active/inactive people you follow.

- **Multiple accounts**: Clients enable you to manage multiple accounts. You can even merge tweets from different accounts into the same timeline.

- **Translation**: Some clients allow you to translate foreign-language tweets.

Hot Tip

Twitter regularly changes the way its software works and some developers may decide not to continue updating their Twitter clients. As a result some of the third-party clients listed in this book may no longer be available.

TOP TWITTER CLIENTS

Thanks to its popularity, there is no shortage of third-party clients that let you manage your Twitter profile. Some of them are extremely sophisticated, whereas others are simple. In addition, while many clients are free, you have to pay for others. Of course, we cannot cover them all in this book, but here are some of the most popular and useful Twitter clients available.

Above: HootSuite is a popular service that allows you to manage multiple social media platforms, including Twitter.

HootSuite

One of the most popular Twitter clients available, HootSuite **(https://hootsuite.com)** allows you to manage numerous social media platforms, not just Twitter. With both a browser-based desktop and mobile app version available, HootSuite lets you schedule tweets, and list and track keywords, as well as monitor mentions, direct messages, favorited tweets, followers and those following you. HootSuite is free, but they do offer paid-for versions with added features aimed at businesses and enterprises.

TweetDeck

Now owned by Twitter, TweetDeck (**https://about.twitter.com/products/tweetdeck**) has become the official desktop client. That does not mean that it is short on features though. With its simple-to-use interface and navigation, it does not take long to learn how to use this powerful Twitter utility. TweetDeck lets you place different followers, topics and trends in

Above: TweetDeck is a free service, allowing you to assess and manage your Twitter activity across multiple accounts.

separate columns. In addition, you can have multiple accounts side by side, as well as seeing images and multimedia in your TweetDeck interface. There is a mobile version too and, best of all, TweetDeck is free.

Tweetings

Another highly popular client, Tweetings (**www. tweetings.net**) is available for iPhone, iPad, Android, Windows and OS X, but you do have to pay for the Mac version (£1.99/$3.00). Features include device synchronization, tweet filters, scheduled tweets and the facility to write more than 140 characters, which makes it ideal for the verbose Twitter user. You can also manage multiple Twitter accounts, and Tweetings has a synchronization feature that ensures you do not see the same tweets on your phone which you have already read on your desktop.

Tweetbot

Only available for iOS users, Tweetbot (**http:// tapbots.com/software/ tweetbot**) costs around £2.99 ($2.99), but you do get plenty of features for

Above: Tweetings features useful options such as device synchronization, tweet filters and scheduled tweets.

your money: multiwindow views, list creation, multiple account management, notifications, timeline sync for multiple devices and a draft feature that gives you the tools you need to create the perfect tweet. There is a desktop Mac version available too, but at about £13.99 ($20), it is perhaps a bit too costly for all but the serious Twitter user.

Above: Tweetbot is not free, but offers features such as multiwindow views, list creation, notifications and timeline sync.

Twitterrific

Another iOS-only app, Twitterrific (**http://twitterrific.com**; around £1.99/$2.99) was one of the first mobile clients for Twitter, but it still holds its own when it comes to features. With the usual multiple account management and timeline synchronization, Twitterrific also has a sophisticated translation feature for translating foreign-language tweets.

Hot Tip

When downloading a Twitter app for your mobile, make sure that it is compatible with your operating system and browser version. Some apps only work with the latest software so you may run into trouble if you have an older phone or tablet.

Above: Twitterfic is an iOS-only app offering added features such as translation of foreign language tweets.

Above: MetroTwit is ideal if you want an easy-to-use client that offers a little more than the standard online Twitter interface.

MetroTwit

A Windows-only desktop client, MetroTwit (**www.metrotwit.com**) is free, easy to navigate and 100 per cent customizable. There is a professional version available at a price (approximately £10/$15), but the basic version offers enough features for most Twitter users, including multiple account management, column groupings, URL shortening and notification management. MetroTwit is ideal for anybody wanting a simple-to-use client that does a little more than the online Twitter interface. The only downside with the free version is that MetroTwit is ad-supported, which might become annoying.

Above: Hibari offers an excellent filtering system, which is great if you find it difficult to sift through the number of tweets you receive.

Hibari

Hibari (**http://hibariapp.com**) offers one of the most comprehensive filtering systems of any Twitter client, enabling you to block keywords, use muting and tweet hiding, as well as search suggestions. The downside is that it is only available for Mac OSX users and costs in the region of £6 ($10), but you can take advantage of a free 14-day trial. If you find it difficult to sift through the number of tweets you receive daily, Hibari could be the answer.

ONLINE TWITTER SERVICES

As well as desktop and mobile Twitter clients, all sorts of online services can also help you to get the most out of Twitter. These offer various facilities, enabling you to do many things that the regular Twitter interface prevents you from doing. Most of these services are free, but will require you to sign in to your Twitter account before you can use them.

Longer Tweets

If you find 140 characters too restrictive, a number of online services enable you to tweet without any word limits.

- **long-tweet.com**: You can write as much as you want in your tweet, as long-tweet will post a link to your full tweet at the end of your allotted 140 characters.

- **TallTweets.com**: Splits your tweets into different parts and posts them all together, avoiding the need for users to click on a link.

- **Long-tweets.com**: Not to be confused with long-tweet.com, Long-tweets converts your message into an image and publishes it on Twitter, so people can read it directly.

Above: Long-tweets.com allows you to produce tweets without word limits, and posts them on Twitter as an image.

Follow Management

If you want to know who has followed you, unfollowed you or who has not posted a tweet in a while, then the following services may help:

Left: Justunfollow is an easy-to-use service when it comes to managing your followers.

- **Justunfollow.com:** Find out who has unfollowed you, who has been inactive and who has added you to their fan page.

- **Wefollow.com:** Lets you find the most suitable people based on keywords; ideal for finding industry experts.

- **Friendorfollow.com:** Similar to Justunfollow, find out who followed you, who unfollowed you and who you are mutual friends with.

Tweet Monitoring

If you want to keep abreast of what people are saying, the following tracking tools may be useful:

- **Tweetreach.com:** Lets you see the impact of your messages by monitoring the reach and exposure of a tweet.

- **Twilert.com:** Receive regular email updates whenever certain keywords are mentioned in tweets; perfect for monitoring your brand.

- **Klout.com:** Another influence-measuring tool that lets you see how prominent you are on social media.

Above: Twilert.com is a useful tracking tool; it sends you email updates when certain keywords are mentioned in tweets.

TWITTER WIDGETS

Apart from a host of clients and services available for interacting with Twitter, there are also numerous Twitter widgets for use with your website or blog. These will allow you to check your tweets from your blog or even let people retweet your blog entries.

- **Tint (www.tintup.com)**: A third-party widget that lets you install your own Twitter feed, other users' feeds and/or posts with a certain hashtag or keyword into your blog or website.

- **Twitter Widget Pro**: A WordPress plugin (ran.ge/ wordpress-plugin /twitter-widget-pro/) that lets you install multiple Twitter feeds into a WordPress blog or website.

Creating and Managing Widgets

Twitter also supplies its own widgets in the Settings/Widgets menu where you can install various feeds, timelines and Twitter searches into your blog or website. This is how to do it.

1. Visit https://twitter.com/settings/widgets, click 'create new' and select the type of widget you want to install (User timeline, Favorites, List, Search or Custom timeline).

2. Fill in the Twitter handle or search query you want to create a widget for.

3. Choose your widget options by ticking the relevant boxes you want to include, such as Exclude replies or Only show top Tweets.

Step 2: To create a User timeline widget, insert the username or Twitter handle (in this case, barackobama) of the feed you wish to install.

4. Customize your widget's link colour, themes and size, then click 'Create widget'.

5. Copy the code that is generated and use it in your website or blog. Most web and blogging software will have an option to view and edit a page's HTML. You should use this mode when pasting in your Twitter widget code.

TWITTER FOR BUSINESS

YOUR TWITTER PROFILE

For a business, the Twitter profile is crucial to get right. It is your opportunity to explain to the Twittersphere who you are and what you do. It is also important if you want to build your brand identity, as it helps to distinguish you from the competition.

TWITTER HANDLE

As with all users on Twitter, a business needs a unique username. Of course, in an ideal world, this should be the name of your company. However, due to Twitter's popularity, another business or user may have already taken your desired name. This means that you will need to come up with an alternative, but it should be something that is identifiable with your brand.

- **What you do**: If you cannot use your company name, choose a username that describes what you do, such as @onlinePCrepairs.

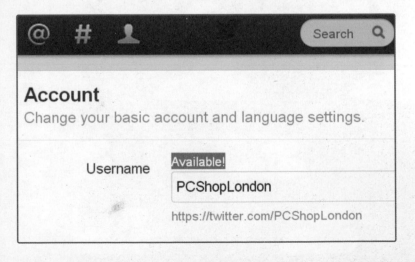

- **Add your location:** If you find that your company name is already in use, adding where you are based might allow you to include your business name in your Twitter handle, e.g. @LondonPCrepairshop.

Left: If your desired username is taken, choose an alternative that enables your customers to identify your business, such as your location.

Using Personal Names

People prefer speaking to actual individuals on Twitter rather than companies. For this reason, it is often a good idea to attach a name to your Twitter handle, such as @PCshopjohn, which can add that personal touch. This is especially effective if you intend on having more than one person tweeting, as each individual can have his or her own Twitter account.

COMPANY NAME

Along with your Twitter handle, you will need to add your company name to your profile. There are no limits to how many people can use the same company name, so you do not have to worry about somebody else having the same business name as you. As your company name is what will appear next to your tweets, choose your normal brand or trading name so that people will be able to identify you.

Right: As an established business, MacWorld are lucky to have been able to use their company name as their Twitter handle; newer businesses may not be so fortunate.

PROFILE IMAGES

Remember that Twitter lets you upload two types of image to your profile, and it is important to take advantage of both.

- **Profile photo**: Use either your company logo or a headshot if you intend to include individual names in your Twitter handle.

- **Header image:** This could also be your logo, albeit enlarged, or it could be a custom design using your branding colours. It could even be an image of one of your products.

PROFILE BACKGROUND

You want your profile page to be as appealing as possible. This means taking advantage of Twitter's many customizable features, including using a profile background. Ideally, you should design your own and upload it. Many companies now specialize in creating bespoke Twitter backgrounds, but if you do it yourself, use your company branding and keep it simple.

Left: When it comes to designing your profile background, follow the example of successful brands, and keep it simple.

COMPANY BIOGRAPHY

Your biography is the one chance you get on Twitter to explain to potential followers who you are. With only 160 characters, you should not waste space by including mission statements or your business philosophy. Keep to the point and explain what you do.

- **Location:** Make sure that you fill in your location so people can find you. Be specific, as your Twitter followers may be from another country and therefore not know your local area.

- **Benefits:** Try to explain the benefits of your products or services, such as convenience, low cost or high quality.

- **Approachable:** Try not to come across as too formal. You want to sound friendly, personable and approachable, yet remain professional.

Keywords

Your Twitter profile is searchable outside of Twitter. In other words, people may come across it when using Google or other search engines. Therefore, try to include a couple of keywords in your profile which will make it as search-engine friendly as possible, thus giving you a better chance of appearing high up in the rankings.

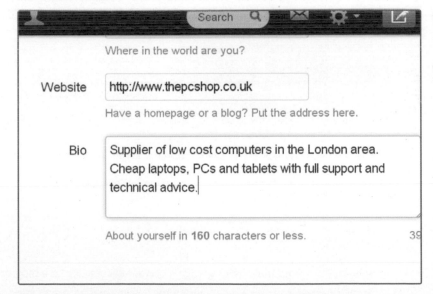

Above: When you write a profile bio, ensure that you include keywords applicable to your business, so that you can be found easily through search engines.

WEBSITE

You need to take advantage of the fact that Twitter lets you include a link in your profile. However, you need to decide where you are going to send your Twitter followers when they click this link.

Hot Tip

Consider creating a specific Twitter landing page, where you can provide information tailored especially to your followers. This will also help you to monitor your web traffic more effectively.

JOHNPAULAGUIAR
THE MONEY DUMMY BLOG

About Me   Getting Started   Build A Blog   Blog Resources

twitter

Welcome Twitter Followers

Welcome to Money Dummy Blog – I'm John Paul Aguiar the Owner and Publisher.

I set this page up to make it easier for you to find my most helpful blog posts having to with everything that is Twitter.

Above: A Twitter landing page is designed specifically for people who have come through to your website from your Twitter profile, such as this money-making blog.

Using Links

Before you include a link, consider your followers and what they will want to see, as well as what you are trying to achieve with your Twitter marketing. Remember that social media is not a sales tool and people may be after more information rather than wanting to place an order. Therefore, rather than sending people to a sales page or your main landing page, consider using a link to a blog or an 'About us' page. Some businesses do include an additional URL in their biography and, although this will not be a clickable link, it can be copied and pasted into a browser.

YOUR TWITTER STRATEGY

If you are using Twitter for business or promotion, you really need to establish a clear strategy. Working out your goals and how best to achieve them is the first step for any successful Twitter campaign.

ESTABLISHING YOUR GOALS

Before you begin tweeting and following, it is worth establishing what you want out of Twitter. Your goals will affect the rest of your strategy, such as the type of people you will follow and the sort of content you will tweet about. All goals need to be realistic, achievable and measurable. For instance, if you would like 10,000 followers, set a deadline for when you want to achieve that number.

Twitter for Business

Your goals will affect how and why you use Twitter. Remember that Twitter is useful in several ways:

- **Brand building**: Twitter is perfect for raising brand awareness and boosting your profile.

- **Customer engagement**: Twitter can provide a platform for customer communication.

- **Promotion**: Twitter is ideal for announcing new products, news and information, as well as bringing traffic to your website.

RESEARCH

Once you know what you want out of Twitter, you need to do your market research to find out what it is that your customers want from you. In order to give customers what they desire, you need to ask what is important to them.

- **Buying influence**: Ask your customers what encourages them to buy products from companies such as yours. Is it price, quality or something else?

- **Reputation**: Before you begin using Twitter to boost your brand, you need to establish what people already think about you. Are there things you need to address? What are your strengths and weaknesses?

- **Competition**: Do not just enquire about yourself; ask how people perceive your competition. Establish what they are doing that you are not.

Hot Tip

In order to assist in your market research, you can include a form on your website for customers to complete.

IDENTIFY YOUR COMMUNITY

Another aspect you need to identify in your research is who your community is. This should not just be your potential customers, but also other people in your industry who may be worth following. If you engage with people on these platforms, it could encourage them to follow you on Twitter.

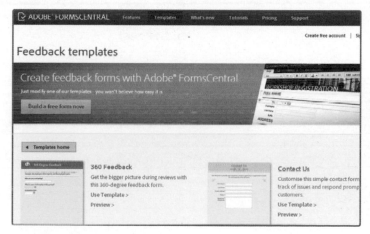

Above: Make use of free templates, such as the one provided by Adobe Acrobat, for hassle-free feedback and market research.

PROMOTING YOUR TWITTER PROFILE

You cannot expect people suddenly to stumble upon your Twitter profile; you need to let them know that you are on there. This may mean including your Twitter details on your website, blog or even your correspondence to customers and suppliers. Some businesses include their Twitter handle with the rest of their contact details, as many people now prefer using social media rather than email or other traditional forms of communication.

Following

Your goals will affect the types of accounts you will follow on Twitter and you need to be selective. People may judge you by the accounts you follow, so do not just follow anybody. This is even more crucial when you start, as

Above: All big companies, such as Tesco, now include Twitter buttons on websites.

it takes time to build up a list of people to follow and people will often look at who you follow to see if you are worth following. Following pop stars or humorous tweeters may not set a good impression with your potential customers.

Who to Follow

For businesses, you want to restrict the people you follow to several categories:

○ **Customers**: When customers follow you, following them back provides positive engagement.

○ **Business associates**: Partners, suppliers and contractors all make for good people to follow.

○ **Trade organizations**: Following professional bodies associated with your industry is a good way to keep up to date with new rules and guidelines.

○ **Professional network**: Following people you know who run other businesses, even in different fields, can also be useful.

○ **News outlets**: Information can be gleaned by following trade journals or websites associated with your industry.

Above: Respected news outlets can be a good way of finding suitable people or organizations to follow

TWITTER CONTENT

The next stage in any Twitter strategy is to work out the type of content you will be sending out. When you plan the sort of things you are going to say on Twitter, take into account your goals as well as what people want to hear. This can often mean a balancing act between promotional content and information that is useful to your followers.

Focusing Content

Generating content that is both beneficial for a business and useful to followers can be difficult. It often means trying to come up with tweets that cover several aspects:

○ **Positivity:** Your tweets should always show your business in a positive light. If somebody tweets something negative about your company, such as a complaint, try to address the concerns openly and honestly.

- **Benefits**: Try to tweet content that will prove helpful for your followers. When promoting, target those aspects of your products or services that could benefit your customers, i.e. low price, quality, convenience, etc.

- **Engagement**: Tweets should be engaging. Make sure that you are producing content that people will want to read.

- **Useful**: Make sure that your tweets provide useful information or answer specific questions put to you by customers.

> ## Hot Tip
> It can often be a good idea to come up with a communication plan. Work out the topic areas you are going to tweet about, and include when and how often you will write about each topic.

TWEET FREQUENCY

The next step to any Twitter strategy is working out how often you will tweet. Tweeting too often can lead people to regard your business as spamming Twitter, especially if all your messages are promotional. On the other hand, not tweeting enough will make people regard you as not worth following. However often you decide to tweet, try to maintain regularity. If you have decided to tweet three times a day, make sure that you stick to that number and try to send your messages out at the same times each day.

Scheduling

Your followers and customers should govern when you send out your messages. If most of them are active during the day, then that is the best time to tweet. However, if you find that your followers are tweeting mainly in the evening, you will want to send out your tweets at that time too. Of course, you do not have to spend all evening on Twitter, as you can use various Twitter clients to schedule your tweets so that they hit the Twittersphere at the right time.

Above: Make use of simple websites, such as futuretweets.com, for scheduling tweets.

TWITTER ACCOUNT MANAGER

Your Twitter strategy should also include who will be sending tweets. As you should stick to your Twitter strategy, and tweet on set topics, it is often a good idea to appoint somebody to oversee your Twitter use. If you have several people tweeting, your Twitter account manager can check that everybody is sending out the right type of content and that you have the right mix of promotional and useful tweets.

Work-based Twitter Culture

Since Twitter is about engagement and communication with your customers, it is a good idea to encourage

> ## Hot Tip
> Twitter is a public space, so you may not want to use it to give financial quotes or take personal information from people, but you can take advantage of direct messages or use it for initial contact with potential customers.

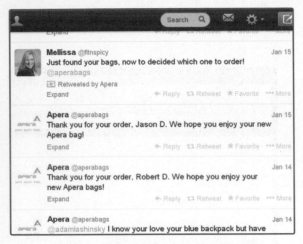

Above: Use Twitter to thank your customers directly for their loyalty, or inform them of bargains or special offers.

employees to use the platform as a means of interaction. Twitter can be used alongside other means of communication, such as the telephone or email, for sending messages to customers, answering queries and helping to address problems.

Twitter Training

If you are going to implement Twitter as part of your work culture, it is important that all employees are familiar with how it works, its benefits and its disadvantages. Simply letting your workforce loose on Twitter without adequate training or supervision could lead to problems, such as somebody unwittingly divulging sensitive information to the Twittersphere. Twitter training is therefore important to ensure that all employees know how best to use the social media platform.

FLEXIBILITY

No matter how well you plan your Twitter strategy, things may not work out how you expected, meaning that you need to be flexible. Make regular assessments of your Twitter strategy. If you have not managed to get the followers you hoped for, or your tweets are not being effective at drawing traffic to your website, think about changing tactic, especially with the type of content you are putting out.

ENGAGING WITH FOLLOWERS

Twitter for business is all about engagement. You need to speak to your customers, reply to their questions, and start and join conversations. Creating and nurturing your followers takes time and effort, but customer engagement can bring plenty of rewards.

CREATING A FOLLOWING

Whatever your goals, obtaining followers is key for a successful Twitter campaign. The only way to achieve this is by producing good-quality tweets. However, getting people to follow you is only half the battle. Keeping them is just as important, which is why you need to engage with people on Twitter.

Your Followers

When you begin on Twitter, you will have little control over who will follow you. You may find that many of your customers and business associates become followers but that you also attract a lot of spam accounts or less desirable Twitter users. When people make the decision to follow a Twitter account, they often look at the list of people already following that person and, therefore, you may want to block certain accounts.

Right: By ensuring your tweets are properly targeted and well written, you will be more likely to attract useful and reputable followers.

Hot Tip

Be careful when blocking accounts or unfollowing people, as the account holder may be a customer who could take exception to it.

SOCIAL MEDIA DIALOGUE

Twitter is about conversation, and just as important as what you are saying in your tweets is how you are saying it: tone is important.

- **Responsive:** Do not just tweet, but also respond to people. Remember that Twitter is about engagement and, therefore, respond to both positive and negative comments.

- **Professional:** As a business, you need to maintain professionalism at all times. Never get into arguments on Twitter or respond to negativity with snide or sarcastic comments.

- **Approachable and genuine:** Try to be as friendly as possible when conversing with people on Twitter. In addition, make sure that you are being honest.

Above: To gauge how others are responding to you and your business on Twitter, click on the Mentions page to view replies, mentions and retweets.

Responding to Tweets

When you respond to comments and questions on Twitter, do so as positively as possible. This is not always easy, especially if somebody has a complaint. However, do not be afraid to apologize and put right things that have gone wrong. You will find that people appreciate candor far more than they appreciate excuses.

Mentions

Make sure that you keep a lookout for mentions by doing searches for your company name, product or service. This can give you a better understanding of your company's reputation and people's perceptions of you. If users mention you (by including the @ symbol with your username), do not be afraid to engage with them, as people will not mind you joining in with the conversation if they have mentioned you. Thank people who say good things about your business and respond positively to those with less favourable opinions.

WRITING TWEETS

Of course, the fundamental aspect of great engagement on Twitter is your tweets. Only by producing good-quality tweets can you build up a following and ensure that people don't unfollow you. Make sure that your content fulfills at least one of the following criteria:

- **Informative**: People like content that benefits them in some way and providing information is one way of achieving this.

- **Helpful**: Be as helpful as possible; show people you care.

- **Engaging**: Although 140 characters is not a lot of space, try to grab people's attention with your tweets. Remember to include images too.

Right: As you are restricted to only 140 characters, you should make use of the odd picture now and again to stand out from the crowd.

EXPANDING YOUR AUDIENCE

Once you start building up a following, you may want to expand your number of followers by using Twitter to seek people out. Use Twitter's suggestions and do not be afraid to search through your competitors' lists of followers, as these may include potential customers.

Finding Potential Customers

Twitter can be a great tool for finding potential customers. While Twitter enables you to converse with people all over the world, it is just as useful for finding people in your area. If you rely on local people for your business, you can use Twitter's advanced search to find users near you.

Hot Tip

You can use Twitter's advanced search function to find local people who are following certain accounts, such as those of your competitors. This can help you further to pinpoint potential customers in your area.

1. Go to Twitter's advanced search page (https://twitter.com/search-advanced).

Written in	Any Language ▼

People

From these accounts	
To these accounts	
Mentioning these accounts	@pcrepairfulham

Places

Near this place	Fulham

Other

Select: ☐ Positive :) ☐ Negative :(☐ Question ? ☐ Include retweets

[Search]

2. In 'Places', enter your location.

3. Add any keywords, account mentions or hashtags to help identify potential customers.

4. Click 'Search'.

Step 2: In the 'Places' box, enter your location.

CREATING A BRAND

Your brand is how other people perceive you, and developing a brand means getting your name associated with what you do. Fortunately, Twitter is one of the most effective tools for helping businesses to build their brands, but only if used correctly.

DEFINING A BRAND

Before you can build your brand on Twitter, you should understand what a brand is. Essentially, a brand is how you would like people to perceive your business and represents several different aspects, which include the following:

○ **What you do:** A brand defines what your business is known for.

○ **Unique:** A brand should also identify your business as being different from other companies in the same industry.

○ **Benefit:** Your brand can define a particular benefit about your business, such as being low cost, high quality, sophisticated or customer orientated.

Above: Apple is one of the world's most iconic brands, associated not just with technology, but also quality, style and sophistication.

Negative Brands

Brands are not just positive, and some businesses develop negative brand associations, such as providing cheap, poor-quality goods or having bad customer service. When you start building a brand, you need to prevent these sorts of perceptions from emerging.

BUILDING BRAND AWARENESS

The first step in building a brand is to get people to identify your company name with what you do. Simply tweeting about your products and services will not do much to boost brand awareness; you need to reinforce your brand identity by engaging with people.

Following

One way of reinforcing your brand identity is by associating yourself with other people on Twitter. This means following those individuals associated with your industry, including the following:

○ **Industry experts:** Follow people and organizations regarded as experts in your field, so that people will find it easier to associate your brand with your industry.

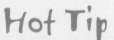

Hot Tip

Learn the commonly used hashtags associated with your products, services or industry, as this can help you to build your brand identity on Twitter.

Above: A good way to reinforce your brand is to follow relevant trade media.

○ **Industry leaders:** Following competitors with established brands and leading companies in your area will help to reinforce your own brand.

○ **Trade bodies:** Follow trade bodies, organizations and trade media to reinforce your brand identity.

Share Your Expertise

Another way of reinforcing your brand presence is by sharing what you know with the Twittersphere. Tweeting useful information will not only attract followers, but also raise awareness of what you do and give you a reputation as being an expert in your field. Encourage people to ask for advice, as this will help to stimulate follows and retweets, and give you plenty of positive brand awareness.

BUILDING BRAND LOYALTY

Once you have started to develop brand awareness, you want to maintain a positive brand image and ensure that people come to you instead of to your competitors.

Maintaining Your Online Presence

As brands need constant reinforcement, you can never relax. The more time you spend reinforcing your brand on Twitter, the more followers you will attract

Above: Get into the habit of, perhaps once a day, searching for tweets mentioning your company, so you can deal with any negative comments immediately.

and, as a result, you will need to dedicate more time to engaging with these new followers. While regular tweets will help to reinforce your brand and keep your potential customers up to date with what your company is doing, building brand loyalty requires you to do other things too.

Public Relations

Many businesses use Twitter to help with customer retention, as this platform gives you the opportunity to search for unhappy customers and address their concerns. This sort of proactive PR can prevent any negative associations with your brand from developing, as well as ensuring that you retain your existing customer base.

Hot Tip

Consider creating your own hashtag unique to your business and use it in your marketing. This can help to make your brand more distinctive and to separate it from others in your industry.

MAXIMIZING YOUR SOCIAL MEDIA POTENTIAL

In order for your brand to get as much exposure as possible, you need to make sure that you are getting the most out of Twitter and your other social media platforms.

- **Advertise your Twitter profile**: Add your Twitter information to your website and blog.

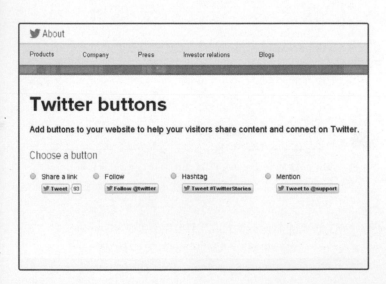

- **Integrate**: Merge Twitter with other social media, as well as including a timeline of your Twitter messages on your website and blog.

- **Include**: Add Twitter buttons to your blog and website to make it easy for people to share your content on Twitter.

Left: You can find Twitter buttons to include on your website at about.twitter.com/resources/buttons.

PROMOTION ON TWITTER

Twitter is not just a great platform for brand building; thanks to its reach, it is also the ideal way to announce new products, promote your business and direct customers to product pages.

USING TWITTER FOR PROMOTION

A single tweet can reach millions of people, making it as potent as TV advertising when it comes to promotion – and tweeting costs nothing. Therefore, if you have something to promote, whether a product or service, Twitter is the ideal tool. However, there are drawbacks to promoting on Twitter, and many people fail to use the platform correctly.

Balance

People will soon tire of you if you just send out tweet after tweet promoting your products or services. Users expect a little promotion, but if that is all you are doing, you will simply cause them to unfollow you. You need to get the correct balance between putting out engaging and useful content, and promotional material. While there is no hard-and-fast rule, it is perhaps not a good idea to send out more than one promotional tweet for every three tweets that contain non-promotional content.

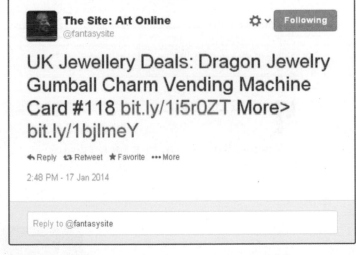

Above: Including a promotional link in your tweet is a great way of attracting your customers to a particular product or offer.

TWEETING PROMOTIONAL CONTENT

With just 140 characters, you cannot use a tweet as a sales pitch. The key to promotion on Twitter is to drive traffic to your website or sales page using a link. However, in order to get people to click your link, you will have to be creative.

- **Benefits:** Rather than try to sell a product in a tweet, outline a main benefit.

- **Tease:** Tempt users to click a link by making them want to know more about your product.

- **Reward:** Offer discounts or freebies to make Twitter users feel privileged.

Hot Tip

Try to include powerful and evocative words, just as headline writers do. The more you can grab a reader's attention, the more likely it is that they will click on your link.

Preview

Kayla Alexander
@KaylaAlex0812

Follow

Astounding Bargains On Face Value Theatre Admission @dealflicks dealflicks.com/?=ox
dealflicks.com

3:35 AM - 10 Jan 2014

Dealflicks
Movie Ticket Deals, Discounts, Offers, & Coupons | Dealflicks

Dealflicks @Dealflicks

Composing Promotional Tweets

A promotional tweet has to centre on your link. Even if you are using a link shortener (*see* page 107), space is going to be at a premium, so you need to compose your message as concisely as possible.

Left: Think before you type: make your promotional tweet sound too good for people to resist.

SOCIAL MEDIA TOOLS

All sorts of tools and Twitter clients can help you with your promotional efforts. Many of these allow you to do things that you simply cannot do using Twitter's main interface.

Using Twitter Clients

Twitter clients have some useful tools for promotion:

- **Scheduling tweets**: Send out your promotional tweets when your Twitter users are most active.

- **Automating tweets**: Automatically generate tweets whenever you have a new product or service to promote, or send automatic responses to tweets when you are not online.

- **Multiple accounts**: Manage several accounts at once.

- **Group**: Separate your customers from your other Twitter followers.

Useful Twitter Clients for Promotion

We have covered some of the best Twitter clients in Chapter Five (*see* pages 174–78), but some of the most useful for promotion include the following:

- **TweetDeck**: Twitter's own desktop client that has plenty of tools useful for promotion.

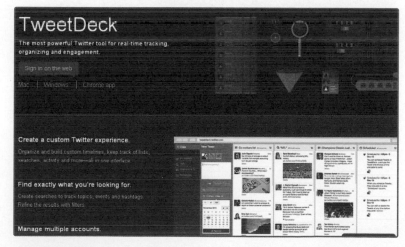

Above: TweetDeck

Above: Hootsuite

Above: Zendesk

○ **HootSuite:** One of the most popular Twitter clients available – and essential for any business managing multiple social media accounts.

○ **Zendesk:** Lets you search for relevant content and import tweets into your business software.

ADVERTISING ON TWITTER

If you really want to reach large numbers of people and tap into the huge audience potential of Twitter, you may consider Twitter advertising. Twitter offers businesses three types of advertisements, so it is important to choose the platform that you think will be most effective for your brand building.

○ **Promoted accounts:** Appear on people's # Discover page as Twitter suggestions of accounts worth following.

○ **Promoted tweets:** Appear on users' timelines with their other tweets.

○ **Promoted trends:** Appear on the list of trending topics.

Promoted Accounts

Promoted accounts are useful for building up a larger following. You can select the people you want to reach according to their interests, location or even gender. This ensures that you are only recommended to users who are likely to want to follow you.

Promoted Tweets

These appear in people's Twitter feed. However, you can target users according to their interests, to specific keywords they have tweeted or to their location, thus ensuring that you are only advertising to people relevant to your brand.

Promoted Trends

Useful for promoting projects or campaigns that you are running, promoted trends mean that your trend will appear at the top of certain users' trending topics. Again, you can target the people who will see your advert and your promoted trend lasts for 24 hours.

How Twitter Advertising Works

Twitter's advertising prices are based on pay-per-action

Above: A promoted tweet is a great way of targeting specific users, according to their interests, about a product or service.

(PPA). This means that you only pay when a person follows your account (promoted accounts), replies, retweets, favorites or clicks a link in your tweet (promoted tweets), or clicks your promoted trend link. This pricing system is based on bidding, which means that you set the maximum amount you are willing to spend per follow or click.

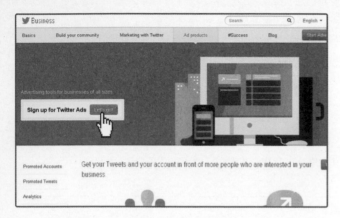

Step 1: Click the Sign up for Twitter Ads button.

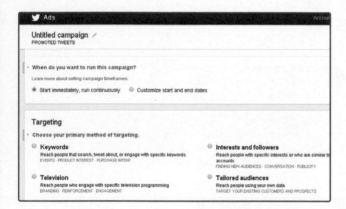

Step 5: You can select how you reach your intended audience, including keywords.

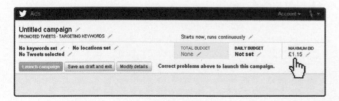

Step 6: Set your bid amount.

There are several stages to advertising on Twitter:

1. Visit https://business.twitter.com/ad-products, and click the Let's go! button, as shown to the left.

2. Select your business location from the drop-down menu and your estimated monthly digital advertising budget.

3. Fill in details of your business and advertisement.

4. Choose the type of Twitter advertisement you would like.

5. Choose how you would like to target your tweets, such as by keywords or interests and followers.

6. Set a daily budget for your campaign (Twitter will stop showing your ads once you hit that figure).

7. Place a click-through bid.

8. Select a date for your promotion to begin.

MEASURING YOUR INFLUENCE

If you are using Twitter as part of a marketing or promotional campaign, you need to know what is working and what isn't, and that means being able to measure your influence.

YOUR TWITTER FOOTPRINT

Measuring your influence on Twitter is not easy. When you send out a tweet, you have no way of knowing how many people are reading it. This can make it difficult to gauge what is the most effective type of content you are putting out. However, there are a few indicators of how much of an impression you are making on Twitter:

Followers

Your influence on Twitter goes beyond how many people are following you, as the quality of your followers is just as important – if not more so. For instance, your followers with the most people following them are going to be more valuable to you when it comes to retweets and mentions than followers with just a handful of people following their accounts.

Above: The more followers your followers have, the better it is for you.

Authoritative Followers

Another aspect to your influence are those followers with the most authority. These people include industry experts, trade organizations and news outlets who not only have a large reach but are also trusted sources of information for people. Therefore, interactions with these account holders will give you more influence in the Twittersphere than retweets and mentions from less authoritative users.

Interactions

Another way of gauging your influence on Twitter is by looking at how many interactions you are receiving. Those tweets that have the most retweets, mentions and are marked as favorite are likely to be your most-read messages. Keep a list of your most successful tweets and see if you can establish what was so effective about them, then try to emulate the same aspects in future tweets.

Above: The Interactions page is a useful tool to help you identify which of your tweets were the most successful.

Hot Tip

You can calculate the exposure that a tweet has received by adding up the number of followers that each person who retweets your content has.

MEASURABLE INFLUENCE

Some aspects of your Twitter influence are quantifiable. Links to your website or sales pages, for example, can be tracked, thus allowing you to establish how effective Twitter is in driving traffic to your website.

Click-through Rates

Monitoring where your traffic comes from is important for any business. With Twitter, you should not only count how many are being directed from the social media platform to your website, but also from which tweets. Those tweets that get the highest click-through rates are going to be the most influential content you have put on to Twitter.

Conversations

Simply sending users from Twitter to your website is only half the battle when it comes to promotion. If people are clicking a link in your tweets and visiting your website but then disappearing again, then your Twitter promotion is not being effective. If your click-through rate is high but your conversation rate is low, your tweets may be misguided and promising things to users that your products or sales page are not delivering.

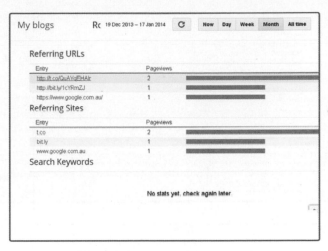

Above: Monitor visitors to your website or blog to see if they have been directed by Twitter, or from elsewhere.

REPUTATION MANAGEMENT

Your influence on Twitter can also be more subjective than just the number of interactions and click-throughs your content is generating. What people are saying about you on Twitter is also important. If there is a lot of negative content about you on Twitter, it could mean that you are failing to engage with people properly, and this can damage your brand. Managing your reputation by addressing customer concerns and negative comments is just as important as promotion if you want to build a brand on Twitter.

> **Hot Tip**
>
> As tweets appear on search engines such as Google, do regular searches to see if yours come up; this can be a good indication that they are being effective at raising your profile.

Customer Retention

Another indication of your influence on Twitter is whether or not your customer retention rate has improved. If you are managing to drive customers to your website from Twitter but they are not returning,

Journalism.co.uk - 13 hours ago

Journalism.co.uk (journalismnews) on Twitter
https://twitter.com/**journalism**news ▼
The latest from **Journalism**.co.uk (@journalismnews). News, digital tools and tips for journalists and publishers from http://t.co/rQev5sEbf4. Editor: Rachel Bartlett ...

Journalism.co.uk (journalismjobs) on Twitter
https://twitter.com/**journalism**jobs ▼
The latest from **Journalism**.co.uk (@journalismjobs). Journalists: sign up for job alerts http://t.co/TR7rc4S4. Recruiters: advertise editorial jobs http://t.co/hAKZtkLl ...

Journalism.co.uk (pressreleases) on Twitter
https://twitter.com/pressreleases ▼
The latest from **Journalism**.co.uk (@pressreleases). Journalists - sign up for free PR alerts http://t.co/liWiPw9N. PRs - publish your press releases directly to ...

womeninjournalism.co.uk
womenin**journalism**.co.uk/ ▼
"Ever since I launched Women in **Journalism** in 1994 it has been at the forefront of the industry. Over those 17 years, women **journalists** from all over the **UK**, ...

Above: Ensure your tweets are doing their bit in promoting your organization, as they are here for trade magazine Journalism.co.uk in a Google search.

then something is going wrong. Use Twitter to see what your customers are saying about you, and put right anything that is going wrong.

MANAGING YOUR INFLUENCE

As you build up a following on Twitter, it can be difficult to manage your influence. Some of those following you will be customers you want to nurture by addressing their concerns or answering their queries, whereas others will be people you converse with on a professional level. One way of making it easier to manage your interactions is to separate your followers and the people you follow into lists. You can keep these private if you wish, so that your followers won't know about it.

- **Customers**: Create a list for customers.

- **Potential customers**: People who have asked a question about your product or service, or made some other enquiry.

- **Trade or professional bodies**: The people you follow to gather information that is useful for your business.

- **Business contacts**: Suppliers, competitors or other people you engage with during your day-to-day business.

- **Personal contacts**: People you chat to on Twitter who have little or nothing to do with your business.

Hot Tip

For more information on how to create lists and make them public or private, *see* pages 77–81.

MEASUREMENT TOOLS

Just as there are all sorts of tools to help with the management of Twitter, you will find a lot of tools that can help you to measure your influence on the social media platform. Some of the most popular are listed in the following sections:

Klout (http://klout.com)

Klout uses analytics from Twitter and other social media to rank you according to your online presence. You receive a 'Klout Score' out of 100, depending on how influential you are. The higher your score, the more social media influence you are wielding.

Simply Measured (http://simplymeasured.com)

It lets you gather all your social media metrics in one place, thus enabling you to analyse and compare your effectiveness across various different platforms.

Twitalyzer (http://twitalyzer.com)

It provides metrics that can help you to examine your Twitter influence. You can analyse all sorts of data in graph form, from the influence of your followers to how effective your promotional campaigns have been.

Above: klout.com

Above: Simply Measured

Above: Twitalyzer

ADVANCED TWITTER

PRIVACY

Twitter is essentially a public platform. This allows you the freedom to say what you like to the world, but also lets anybody see your tweets and profile, so it is worth understanding a little about privacy on Twitter and how you can protect yourself against unwanted attention.

WHAT IS PRIVATE?

The big advantage of Twitter compared to other social media platforms is that you can follow anybody you like. You do not have to know the person and, unless a user has their tweets protected, you do not need permission to follow them. This openness does come with its downside, as not only can you follow anybody, but also anybody can follow you. This means that your tweets, profile and interactions are completely public.

Tweeting to the World

As a result of Twitter's openness, some people have found that the things they have said have got them into trouble. It is not just your friends and followers who see your tweets – your employer, parents, local authorities and even the police can too.

The Golden Rule of Tweeting

Perhaps the golden rule for anybody using Twitter should be: never say anything in a tweet that you would not feel comfortable saying in public. This means that you should never write anything that you would not want your mother, employer or the authorities to see. Additionally, you should never say anything to somebody on Twitter that you would not feel comfortable saying to their face.

SHARING INFORMATION

Since tweets are public, any information you share is visible to the world. Moreover, your Twitter profile is public too. This means that anything in your biography can be viewed by anyone. For this reason, it is perhaps best to avoid revealing certain personal details.

- **Address:** Unless you are a business, never reveal your address in a tweet or Twitter profile.

- **Phone number:** Never reveal your phone number on Twitter, as anybody could get hold of it.

- **Financial information:** Never send anybody your credit card or bank account number, even by direct message.

- **Images:** Never post compromising pictures in a tweet or photographs of people who may take exception to the whole world seeing them.

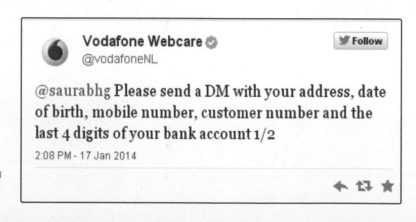

Vodafone Webcare ✓
@vodafoneNL

▶ Follow

@saurabhg Please send a DM with your address, date of birth, mobile number, customer number and the last 4 digits of your bank account 1/2

2:08 PM - 17 Jan 2014

Right: It is best to avoid sending personal information via Twitter, even to reputable companies, as requested here.

PRIVACY SETTINGS

You can, of course, alter certain privacy settings on Twitter (*see* page 89). This lets you control who can access your tweets.

- **Location**: If you do not want people to know where you are from, or where you currently are, you can switch this off.

- **Protected tweets**: Allows only people who you have approved to see your tweets.

- **HTTPS only**: Helps to protect your account information by using a secure and encrypted connection. See below for further information.

> **Hot Tip**
>
> Make sure that you change your Twitter password regularly. This will make it harder for anybody to gain access to your account if your details are ever compromised.

HTTPS Only

HTTPS (Hypertext Transfer Protocol Secure) provides more security than standard HTTP by preventing any interception of your data as it goes from your computer to Twitter. By selecting HTTPS Only, Twitter will always log you in using HTTPS. However, some third-party applications and older browsers do not offer HTTPS support, so selecting this option means you will no longer be able to access Twitter using these platforms.

Going Private on Twitter

When you adjust your privacy settings on Twitter, not only will it drastically reduce the number of followers you receive, but also, no privacy system

Password
Change your password or recover your current one.

Associate your mobile phone with your Twitter account for enhanced security. Learn more.

Current password [••••••••]
Forgot your password?

New password [••••••••••••] Weak

Verify password [ ]

[Save changes]

Left: For safety's sake, it's a good idea to update your Twitter password from time to time.

is completely infallible. While you may only intend for certain people to see your tweets, you have no way of knowing whether those people have shared the information you have given out.

HOW TWITTER USES YOUR INFORMATION

When you register for a Twitter account, you will be required to give certain information. Additionally, every time you tweet, follow or interact on the platform, certain details are stored. The information that you divulge on Twitter falls into three different categories: some is kept private, while other types are made public.

- **Private:** Information that Twitter never divulges; this includes your password, phone number and email address. However, Twitter may use these details to send you marketing information.

- **Public:** Your name, username and biographical information are made public. These are not only visible to other Twitter users, but also to those who do not have an account, as they will be able to see public profiles.

- **Interactions:** Messages you tweet, lists you create, people you follow and tweets you have retweeted are made public unless you protect them in your privacy settings.

Cookies

As with other websites, Twitter uses cookies to monitor how you are using its service. A cookie is a small data file stored on your computer's hard disk and allows Twitter to save your settings.

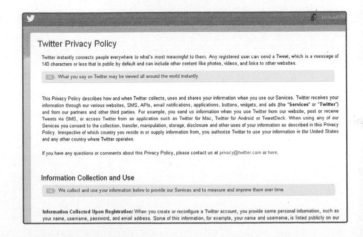

Above: For detailed information on Twitter's privacy policy, look at twitter.com/privacy.

Allowing Twitter Email and Phone Access

While Twitter never discloses your email address or phone number, it can identify people who already have this information, such as those you speak to by email. It uses this information to make suggestions for who to follow, but you can turn this option off in your privacy settings (*see* page 89).

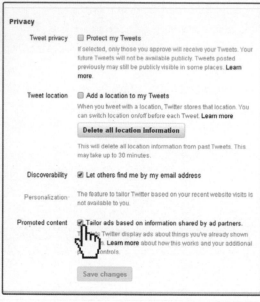

Above: To turn off tailored advertisements, uncheck the box next to Promoted content in your account settings.

Hot Tip

Turning off tailored adverts does not mean that you will not see promoted content on your Twitter feed; instead, the adverts you see will be random and not tailored specifically to you.

What is Shared?

Twitter will never divulge your private information to third parties, but it does share some of your public information and your usage of its website. For instance, third-party apps that integrate with Twitter require certain details stored in your cookies to be able to integrate with your account, while Twitter uses this information to provide you with tailored adverts. You can, however, turn off tailored ads in your privacy settings by unchecking the 'Promoted content' box.

CYBER-STALKING

While Twitter is a public forum where people have the freedom to express themselves, everybody is entitled to a certain level of privacy and respect. Although rare, some people have come across a Twitter user who has harassed or bullied them online. Harassment on Twitter can involve the following:

- **Abuse**: Persistent abusive tweets aimed at or about you.

- **Threats**: Somebody is making threats of violence towards you.

- **Privacy**: Somebody is revealing private information about you.

Handling Twitter Harassment

If you suffer problems because somebody is harassing you on Twitter, there are steps you can take:

1. Block and unfollow the user who is being abusive towards you.

2. Go to https://support.twitter.com/forms/abusiveuser to report the abuse.

3. Fill in the form, including the Twitter handle of the offender, and links to any abusive tweets and details of when they were sent.

Hot Tip

Although Twitter may block the IP address of an abusive tweeter, this person may find a way to open up another account. If problems persist, contact the police.

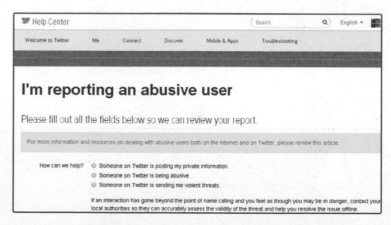

Above: Twitter's Help Center gives you more information on how to deal with abusive behaviour.

TWITTER AND CHILDREN

While the majority of people on Twitter are adults, many youngsters have signed up for accounts. Twitter is a great platform for teenagers to socialize and uncover information, but being on such a public forum does pose risks to them, especially in relation to bullying and unwanted attention from adults.

Protecting Children

If your child is using Twitter, it is worthwhile taking a few precautions to ensure that it is a safe environment for them to be in:

1. Encourage your child to protect their tweets so that only their friends can see what they are saying.

2. Monitor your child's online activity. Make sure that you know to whom they are speaking on Twitter and are aware of the relationships they are forming.

Hot Tip

Twitter stipulates that users must be over the age of 13 to register for an account. However, in reality, it has practically no way of enforcing this policy or knowing the true age of its users.

3. Make sure that your child is aware that what they say on Twitter can be viewed by anyone, including their teachers and school friends.

4. Report any bullying or inappropriate tweets sent to your child to Twitter and/or the authorities.

TWITTER SECURITY AND PRIVACY TIPS

We have compiled a few tips to help you keep your Twitter account safe, and avoid any potential security and privacy issues.

○ **Public computers**: Make sure that you log off from your Twitter account when using a public or work computer.

○ **Links**: Avoid clicking on links from users you do not know, as these could be from spammers redirecting you to a phishing or malware webpage.

○ **Information**: Be guarded about the sort of information you reveal on Twitter. Even something as innocuous as your birth date can be used by people with malicious intent.

○ **Emails**: If you receive emails from Twitter, avoid clicking on any links, as you may have received a bogus message leading you to a fake Twitter page.

Above: Even if you receive a genuine Twitter email (as pictured), be aware that fake Twitter emails are frequently sent in order to trick you into divulging personal information.

TWITTER AND THE LAW

Since its inception in 2007, the controversy created by Twitter has grown almost as much as its popularity. Many news stories around Twitter have centred on libel and other legal issues, which all users need to be aware of.

CITIZEN JOURNALISM

Until the appearance of Twitter, the average person had little chance to reach as many people with their views and opinions as they can now. In essence, Twitter has turned everybody into a publisher. However, while journalists from traditional media undergo training so that they understand what can be reported in newspapers and magazines, few people on Twitter have such a working knowledge of the law.

Responsibility

Although Twitter is a new medium, it is still governed by the same laws that rule traditional publications. Many people who have got into trouble on Twitter often did not realize that what they were doing was against the law. However, ignorance is not an excuse and, as a Twitter user, you need to understand that you are responsible for everything that you tweet.

Left: Twitter is governed by the same laws as mainstream media, so before tweeting anything sensitive or controversial, make sure that you understand fully the possible legal repercussions of doing so.

Global Platform

The law differs from country to country. Therefore, what may be perfectly legal to say in one place could be against the law in another. For instance, compared to citizens in the UK, US citizens have far more freedom – under the first amendment – when it comes to commenting on court cases, or making statements about people or organizations. Since Twitter is a global platform, it is quite possible for you to be in breach of another country's law and, although there has not yet been anything as dramatic as an extradition order placed because of a tweet, this is not out of the question.

Republication

Another crucial aspect of the law governing publishing is that you do not necessarily have to be the creator of an illegal tweet to run foul of the law. Retweeting something that someone else has said could result in legal action against you.

> ## Hot Tip
> Remember that tweets can last for ever. Therefore, if you said something a long time ago that contravened a law, yet suffered no repercussions, it may still come back to haunt you.

#withHandycam: bit.ly/LkXm4H
Expand   ← Reply ⟲ Retweet ★ Favorite ••• More

Press Gazette @pressgazette   Jan 18
Playboy sues Harper's Bazaar over Kate Moss photos ow.ly/slfh9
Expand   ← Reply ⟲ Retweet ★ Favorite ••• More

Our Journalism @OurJournalism   Jan 18
INSTAGRAM: Thousand people affected by the flood, hopefully we deliver the truth and help inform people.. #ip... bit.ly/Kf3ds5
Expand   ← Reply ⟲ Retweet ★ Favorite ••• More

Our Journalism @OurJournalism   Jan 18
INSTAGRAM: #insta_global #instablackanwhite #igworldclub_award #ig_turkey #instamood #instagramtürkiye #ig_str... bit.ly/1gZMPXa
Expand   ← Reply ⟲ Retweet ★ Favorite ••• More

Above: Retweets mean that something said in the heat of the moment may never truly vanish from the Twitterverse.

TWIBEL

One of the most reported legal issues affecting Twitter is libel. There have been some high-profile incidents of libel on Twitter in recent times and, in fact, this has become such a big issue that a new term has been coined: 'Twibel'.

Defamation

Libel is part of the law of defamation, which has two forms:

- **Slander**: When you say something that is defamatory.

- **Libel**: When you write, publish or broadcast something defamatory, such as in a tweet.

Libellous Comments

In law, libel is defined as something that is both untrue and causes 'substantial harm' to an individual's reputation. This may include causing somebody to be the subject of hatred, ridicule or contempt, lowering their standing in society, encouraging exclusion of that person, or imputing a lack of professional skill or efficiency.

Libel Defence

It is notoriously difficult and expensive to defend against libel. Also, while it is usually a civil offence, thus not resulting in a criminal conviction, a libel case can result in extremely large fines and court expenses. However, there are some defences of libel in UK law that may be applicable to using Twitter:

○ **Fair comment**: An honestly held opinion based on provable facts. This defence is now referred to as 'honest comment'.

○ **Justification**: You cannot be sued for libel if the statement you have made is true (and provably so).

○ **Privilege**: It is not libel if the statement was made in court or Parliament and you simply repeated what was said in these arenas.

○ **Innocent dissemination**: Where a person or organization has little control over the publication of a libellous comment. Twitter can claim such a defence, as it cannot be expected to moderate every tweet, but users cannot.

Twibel in the News

Perhaps the most notable case of twibel in the UK was when a rumour began circulating on Twitter falsely linking Lord McAlpine, a former politician, with sex abuse claims. Sally Bercow, the wife of the Speaker of the House of Commons, tweeted: 'Why is Lord McAlpine trending? *innocent face*'. In a subsequent court case, a judge deemed Mrs Bercow's tweet libellous and she agreed to pay damages. In addition, over 500 users who retweeted what she had said were pursued for libel. These people were eventually allowed to settle the matter by making a £25 charitable donation.

Hot Tip

The law has now been changed to force website operators, such as Twitter, to remove potentially libellous comments and hand over the details of anonymous users to the authorities.

CONTEMPT OF COURT

Unlike countries such as the United States, the UK has strict rules about what can be said with regard to court cases. Twitter users who tweet or retweet comments about them can end up in contempt, which can result in a prison sentence.

Above: The tweet pictured here resulted in libel action against the user and fines to those who retweeted it, so always think before you tweet.

Contempt in Tweets

In the UK, a tweet can be considered in contempt of court in several ways:

- **Court cases:** Any comments regarding the innocence or guilt of a person during an ongoing court case – or divulging any facts relating to the case that were not revealed in court – could be considered contempt.

- **Identification:** It is contempt to reveal the identity of a person protected by a court order, such as the victim of a sex crime or a minor.

- **Injunctions:** Divulging the details of anything protected by an injunction is contempt. In some cases, even naming a person who has taken out an injunction could be considered contempt.

- **Jurors:** Users who try to contact witnesses or defendants on social media or discuss a court case can be jailed for contempt.

HARASSMENT

Twitter can get people into trouble in other ways too. Harassment is a criminal offence in the UK and this extends to Twitter. A way to establish whether harassment has taken place is to consider: 'if a reasonable person in possession of the same information would think the course of conduct amounted to or involved harassment'.

Above: The footballer Ryan Giggs became infamous after the contents of the super-injunction he had placed (now lifted) was discussed on Twitter.

Malicious Tweets

Sending out tweets containing false information with the purpose of damaging a person's business or reputation may be considered malicious falsehood. This is distinct from defamation, but carries financial penalties just as severe.

Hot Tip

Accountant Paul Chambers was convicted of menace after he tweeted: 'I am blowing the airport sky high' in frustration at an airport closure. His conviction was overturned after a judge conceded that most people would not regard the tweet as being serious.

twitter

Crap! Robin Hood airport is closed. You've got a week and a bit to get your shit together, otherwise I'm blowing the airport sky-high!!

pauljchambers
Paul Chambers

Menace

In the UK, Twitter is governed by the 2003 Communications Act, which prohibits the sending of grossly offensive, obscene or menacing content. However, this is highly subjective, as what one person may find menacing or grossly offensive may be considered by another to be a joke.

Threats

Any tweet that makes a threat of violence, or encourages somebody else to commit an act of violence or unlawful conduct, could result in a criminal conviction. Tweeting anything that is intimidating could also lead to a civil case for compensation if a person can prove that it caused psychological damage, loss or suffering.

INTELLECTUAL PROPERTY

Intellectual property includes creative works (such as poetry, books and song lyrics), and tweets can result in breaches of intellectual property law. However, a breach of copyright is usually only considered if a substantial part of a work has been copied and, as a tweet only consists of 140 characters, it is highly unlikely that this could be proved. Bear in mind, though, that copyright law also protects images, so you cannot take a picture posted on Twitter and use it without the owner's permission.

Trademarks and Hashtags

Trademarks are protected by law to prevent false association with products and services. Due to the prevalence and use of hashtags on Twitter, there is a risk that using a trademarked name preceded by the # symbol could result in a trademark infringement, especially if this causes people to associate the user who tweeted with the product or service.

Impersonation

It is common on Twitter for people to open accounts under the name of celebrities and public figures. However, this could constitute fraud if the latter suffered any financial loss because of the false Twitter account, or if the account holder obtained money as a result of the pretence.

Right: Any image posted on Twitter is protected under copyright law and cannot be reused without first seeking the owner's permission to do so.

DATA PROTECTION

The law in the UK protects people's personal information. Tweets revealing somebody's personal details, especially if they were obtained in the context of a work environment, could result in breach of the Data Protection Act, which carries a large fine and even a criminal conviction. However, the law is unclear as to whether simply revealing someone's personal details outside of the employment context, such as a friend's address, would constitute a breach of Data Protection. Basically, in order to be on the safe side, it is probably best never to divulge any information about somebody else without their permission.

Confidential Information

Contractual obligations may also affect what you can tweet about. Revealing any information on Twitter without your employer's agreement could not only lose you your job but also result in a case brought against you for damages. Furthermore, information that could be used to gain a financial benefit could result in a criminal conviction, as it could constitute 'insider trading', i.e. whenever information pertaining to a business is used as an advantage when trading in shares or stocks.

TAKING TWITTER FURTHER

Once you have got to grips with Twitter, you may want to take your usage beyond just tweeting, retweeting and following. Twitter can be a useful tool for finding out information, and has uses that extend beyond social networking.

TWITTER AS A SEARCH ENGINE

With so many users and so much content tweeted each day, Twitter contains a wealth of information. Essentially, you can look at Twitter as a mini internet, with each tweet as a micro webpage with images, links and useful material. As with the full-size internet, finding what you want means using a search engine. Twitter's advanced search, while not as sophisticated as Google or the other internet engines, still has plenty of capabilities, which can help you to find the information you need.

Using Advanced Search

In order to take advantage of Twitter search, you really need to move away from the standard search bar and use the advanced search (http://www.twitter.com/search-advanced). This includes all sorts of parameters and is particularly useful when you combine them in your searches.

Right: Twitter's Advanced Search, when used correctly, can find information above and beyond everyday tweets.

Advanced Search Parameters

- **All of these words**: If you type in a keyword phrase, Twitter will find all tweets containing each word within it.

- **This exact phrase**: A bit like using quotes in Google, as Twitter will only bring up results with tweets containing the entire phrase.

- **Any of these words**: A more general search for finding tweets containing one or more of the words you entered.

- **None of these words**: Lets you filter out words and is especially useful if your keyword is associated with different subjects.

- **These hashtags**: Lets you search for content that contains specific hashtags.

Hot Tip

If you add 'http' to the 'All of these words' category, you will get tweets that only contain links, which is useful for finding further information on topics.

- **Written in**: Lets you define which language the tweet is written in.

- **From these accounts**: This is where you can filter tweets that are written by a specific user – useful for searching through the content of Twitter users who have tens of thousands of tweets under their belts.

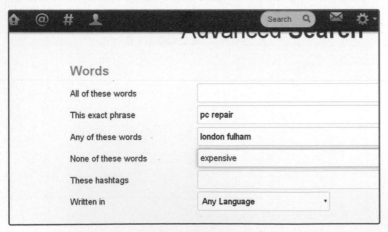

Above: By entering detailed search terms, the results of your search can be extremely accurate.

- **To these accounts**: Lets you find tweets sent to a specific user.

- **Mentioning these accounts**: Tweets that mention a user. Useful for businesses searching for mentions of their name or those of their competitors.

- **Near this place**: Lets you find tweets sent from or near a particular location – great for finding content written by local people.

- **Other**: Allows you to filter tweets containing certain emoticons, retweets or questions.

Taking Advantage of Advanced Search

Twitter Advanced Search lets you target not only specific information, but also specific types of users. For instance, doing a keyword search and ticking 'Question' in 'Other' will bring up tweets from people

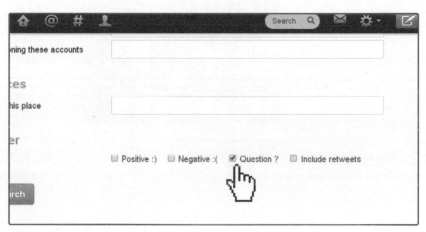

Above: Twitter's Advanced Search facility allows you to search not only for answers, but also for questions.

asking a question related to your keywords. This could be a question that you could answer, thus making this a useful way of finding new followers.

Expert Search

Advanced Search is also a useful tool for finding experts in a particular field. Many media professionals now use Twitter when they want some expert comment, as this is a much easier way to find people with specific knowledge than trawling through the phone book or calling certain organizations, such as universities. Since so many people tweet from their mobiles, it is also a lot simpler to find contactable people on Twitter, especially if you are asking a question out of normal office hours.

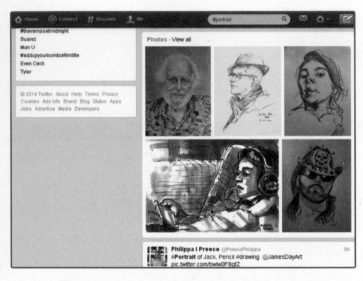

Above: Artists use the hashtag #portrait to show off their portraiture work.

TWITTER AS A PORTFOLIO

Twitter is not only a useful way of promoting your work; it can also be used as a mini portfolio. Writers, artists and designers can tweet links to their work and associate a unique hashtag to it, thus storing a complete portfolio in their tweets section. They can then direct a prospective employer to the hashtag, who will be able to see a list of tweets that link to all the relevant work.

Hot Tip

When you create your own hashtag, make sure that you do a search to check that it is not already in use. Also, steer clear of anything that looks similar to another hashtag in order to avoid the problem of typos.

CONFERENCING AND Q&A ON TWITTER

Forget expensive software – Twitter provides a simple solution for organizing conferences and Q&A sessions. If you assign a unique hashtag to an event, you can send it to a list of people and therefore will be able to set up a conference or hold a Q&A session. This can allow dozens (or even hundreds) of people to take part in the same event, where they can ask questions and read responses.

TWITTER TESTIMONIALS

Tweets are also useful as references and testimonials. Before Twitter, if a business wanted an endorsement from a particular customer, they would have to contact that person and ask them to say something nice. Now a business can search for tweets where people are saying good things about their product or service and simply embed them into a website or blog (for more on embedding tweets, *see* page 144).

Above: Positive Twitter testimonials are frequently used by businesses as a promotional tool on their websites.

MULTIPLE TWITTER ACCOUNTS

For many Twitter users, one account is simply not enough. You may decide that you want an account for work, one for personal contacts and perhaps one for any specialist interest you may have. Fortunately, Twitter has no rules prohibiting the creation of more than one account; there are, however, a few restrictions:

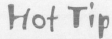

You can use a Twitter client, such as TweetDeck or HootSuite, to manage multiple accounts.

- **Email:** You need a unique email address for each Twitter account, as an address can only be associated with one Twitter account.

   Right: TweetDeck is a useful way of managing multiple Twitter accounts.

- **Logging in**: You cannot log into more than one Twitter account at any one time from the same browser. However, you can use a second browser or a private browsing session window.

- **Followers**: Sadly, there is no way to export followers, so if you start a new account, you will have to begin building up a new following.

- **Username**: You can use the same real name for each account, but not the same twitter handle, which has to be unique.

DEACTIVATING A TWITTER ACCOUNT

If you have tired of Twitter – or have several accounts, one of which is no longer in use – you can deactivate it. Twitter automatically deactivates accounts after six months of inactivity. However, if you want to remove your profile and tweets immediately, you can do so.

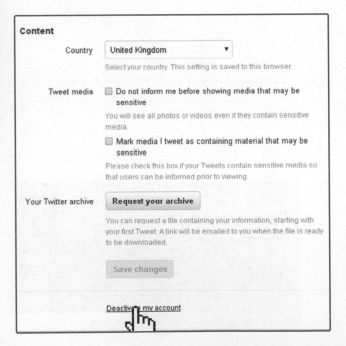

1. Log into the account you want to deactivate at twitter.com (you cannot deactivate an account using an app or Twitter client).

2. In the 'Account settings' pane in Settings (gear wheel icon and Settings), click 'Deactivate my account' at the bottom of the page.

Step 2: Click the 'Deactivate my account' link in your Account settings pane.

3. Read the account deactivation information. This will explain that, although your account will be removed in a few minutes, some content may still be visible on search engines for a while.

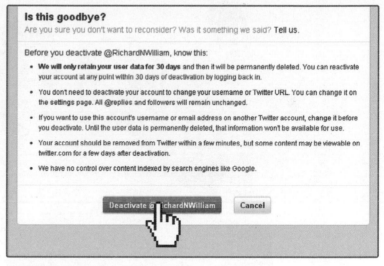

Is this goodbye?
Are you sure you don't want to reconsider? Was it something we said? **Tell us.**

Before you deactivate @RichardNWilliam, know this:

*   **We will only retain your user data for 30 days** and then it will be permanently deleted. You can reactivate your account at any point within 30 days of deactivation by logging back in.
*   You don't need to deactivate your account to change your username or Twitter URL. You can change it on the settings page. All @replies and followers will remain unchanged.
*   If you want to use this account's username or email address on another Twitter account, change it before you deactivate. Until the user data is permanently deleted, that information won't be available for use.
*   Your account should be removed from Twitter within a few minutes, but some content may be viewable on twitter.com for a few days after deactivation.
*   We have no control over content indexed by search engines like Google.

[Deactivate @RichardNWilliam]   [Cancel]

4. Click 'Deactivate'.

5. Enter your password to confirm that you want to deactivate your account.

Step 4: Press the blue Deactivate button to deactivate your account.

Hot Tip

If you change your mind after deactivating an account, you can reactivate it again within 30 days, as Twitter keeps all your details for this time. However, after 30 days, your account is deleted for ever.

TWITTER LIMITS AND RESTRICTIONS

Few people are ever faced with Twitter's restrictions. However, for those who become hardened users, there are limits, set daily, to prevent downtime and errors. If you reach one, you will receive an error message and may have to wait a day for the limit to be reset.

- **Direct messages**: You can only send 250 DMs each day.

- **Tweets**: You can send 1,000 tweets per day, although the limit is broken down into hourly restrictions (about 41 tweets an hour), which include retweets and replies.

- **Email**: You can only change your account email four times in any one hour.

- **Following**: You can only follow 1,000 accounts per day. You may also be prevented from following more than 2,000 accounts in total, depending on how many followers you have.

API Limits

Third-party software, such as Twitter clients, use application programming Interface (API) to integrate with Twitter. However, Twitter restricts the number of interactions to 150 API calls an hour. Every search, follow, tweet, retweet or direct message counts as an API call.

Uh-oh! You're being rate-limited!

While we appreciate your enthusiasm, in order to control abuse, we limit how often you can search.

For locations where many people share the same IP address (e.g., corporations and conferences), our rate limits may be too strict. If you believe you are using Twitter search normally, please let us

Above: If you are using an API, such as a phone app, to access Twitter, you will be notified when you have reached your search limit.

SOME TWITTER HINTS

Despite all the information already provided in this book, there are a few tips and tricks we have not yet covered. Here are a few things that might help you along the way.

- **Ampersand:** Fine in tweets, but avoid using the & symbol in your Twitter profile, as some platforms do not display it properly.

- **Tweet length:** Although you have 140 characters, try to keep your tweets below 125, as this makes it easier for people to retweet and add comments.

- **Serial tweeting:** Try to make each tweet a complete message, as people may not see your tweets all together or in the correct order. If you do tweet in several parts, use a hashtag to make it easier for people to find all the messages.

- **Links:** Avoid always placing a link at the end of a tweet. Positioning them in the middle or at the beginning encourages more click-throughs.

- **Have fun:** Don't let Twitter become a chore or a burden. If you are not enjoying it but still feel compelled to tweet, it may be time to take a break.

TROUBLESHOOTING

Sometimes on Twitter, things go wrong or, for some reason, you cannot accomplish what you want. Often, the solution is fairly simple, which is why we have prepared these common troubleshooting tips.

LOGIN

The most common reason for being unable to log in is that you are entering incorrect details. It can be quite easy to misremember or mistype either your username or password. Furthermore, passwords on Twitter are case sensitive, so it is always worth checking that Caps Lock is not on.

Hot Tip

You can log into Twitter using either your username (Twitter handle) or email address. If you cannot log in using one method, try the other.

Step 1: By clicking on the 'Forgot password?' link, you will be able to reset a forgotten password.

Lost Password

If you have recently changed your password and now can no longer remember your new one, do not worry; it is easy to reset your password again.

1. On the login screen, click the 'Forgot password?' link.

2. Either enter your email address or phone number (if registered to Twitter), or enter your Twitter handle (username).

3. Click 'Submit'.

4. Check your email account, as Twitter will have sent you a new password. If you cannot find it, check your spam folder, as your spam filter may have intercepted it.

Step 3: Click 'Submit' once you have entered either your email address, phone number or username (as here).

Compromised Accounts

If you think that your Twitter account has been compromised, i.e. somebody else has obtained your password, or tweets or direct messages that you didn't write have been sent from your account, the first step is to reset your password. Next, you should cancel all third-party access to clients, websites and apps, as one of these could have been the reason your account was compromised.

1. Visit the 'Apps' section in Settings (gear wheel menu and 'Settings').

2. Click 'Revoke access' next to each client, app or web service.

Step 2: Click 'Revoke access' to cancel third-party access to apps if you think your account has been compromised.

3. Sign into your trusted clients, apps and services using your new password.

Suspended Accounts

Twitter occasionally suspends accounts if it believes that users have violated its terms and conditions. If your account has been suspended unfairly (for example, because it was compromised), you can appeal the decision by visiting https://support.twitter.com/forms/general?subtopic=suspended and filling in the appeal form.

ACCOUNT ISSUES

One of the most common problems that people have with Twitter is when the link between their account and their email address is broken. This can happen for a number of reasons:

- **Changed email**: You may have a new email address and no longer have access to the old one.

- **Hacked account**: A malicious user may have reassigned the email address linked to your Twitter account.

- **Entered an incorrect email**: If you have misspelled your email address or entered it incorrectly, you will not be able to confirm your Twitter account and gain full access.

- **Email confusion**: Many of us have multiple email addresses these days, and it can be easy to forget which one you used to sign up to Twitter.

Twitter Email

If you want to change your email or check which account is linked to Twitter, log in using your username and go to the 'Account' menu in Settings. If you cannot log in, click 'Forgot Password?' and enter any possible email address. You will see a confirmation message when you enter the one linked to a Twitter account.

Above: If you enter an invalid email address, a red error message comes up (as here); when you enter a linked email account, the error message turns green and says Looks Good.

Email Confusion

Some people occasionally receive an email saying that the address has been used to sign up to Twitter. Often, this is simply a mistake by somebody mistyping their email address and you can remove the email from the account easily.

1. Click 'Not my account' in the email sent by Twitter.

2. You will be taken to a web page where you can click the 'I did not sign up for this account' button to remove your email address from the account.

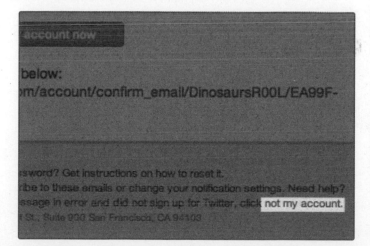

Step 1: If you get emails for a Twitter account you didn't sign up for, click the 'Not my account' link to remove your email from that specific Twitter account.

Above: To change your username at any time, go to your account settings and type a new one into the Username box.

Usernames

Usernames can cause several problems when using Twitter:

- **Forgotten username:** Twitter handles are easily forgotten. However, you can always log into your Twitter account using your email address.

- **In use:** Since usernames are unique, the one you really want may already be taken. Try using underscores or adding numbers if you really want a certain Twitter handle.

- **Changing username:** If you want to change your username, you can do so at any time in 'Account' settings.

> ## Hot Tip
> Despite the use of the @ symbol, Twitter handles are not like email addresses, so do not contain words or characters before the @.

PROFILE IMAGE ISSUES

Although creating a profile is normally straightforward, some people do occasionally have issues uploading images. This is normally caused by one or more of the following reasons:

- **File type:** Twitter only accepts images in JPEG, GIF (non-animated) and PNG formats. If your picture is in a different format, use image editing software (such as Paint) to save it as another file type.

- **Image size:** A profile image has to be under 2 MB (5 MB for header Images). Files larger than this will not be uploaded so, again, use editing software to shrink the image.

- **Outdated system:** An old internet browser or operating system may cause some issues when uploading an image. Either update your software or try a new browser.

TWEETING ISSUES

Some people experience a few issues when sending tweets. However, this is normally caused by something simple.

Error Messages

Twitter does not like people sending the same tweet too often so, after sending a repeated tweet, you may receive the error message: 'Whoops! You already tweeted that...'. In this case, you can either add 'ICYMI' (in case you missed it) before the tweet, or try sending the repeated tweet later on.

Replies and Mentions

If your replies and mentions are not reaching the right people, there may be a mistake in how you have composed the username.

Above: Sending a tweet that contains exactly the same text as you have included in another recent tweet will result in Twitter sending you this Whoops! message.

- **Symbols and spaces:** Make sure that there are no symbols or spaces in or after the username, such as full stops.

- **@ sign:** This has to be connected to the username without a space. However, it cannot be connected to the preceding word and therefore needs a space before it.

Above: Remember: a Twitter handle with a space after @ won't work!

Protected tweets: If you have protected tweets, you cannot reply to or mention somebody who is not on your list of approved followers.

Hashtags

Many of the same rules relevant for usernames apply to hashtags too: you cannot have words or symbols preceding the # sign, and you cannot have symbols or spaces following it.

Direct Messages

The most common issues with direct messages include the following:

- **Cannot send:** You can only send a DM to somebody who is following you.

- **Not receiving:** You can only receive a DM from somebody you are following.

- **Missing DMs:** If the sender deletes a DM, it will disappear from both his or her inbox and yours. Twitter also only displays the last 100 DMs (sent and received) in your inbox.

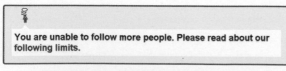

Above: Once you've hit 2,000 followers, you will receive this error message and be subject to follower restrictions.

FOLLOWING ISSUES

If you find you cannot follow another Twitter user, this may be due to one of three reasons:

- **Follow limit:** You can follow 2,000 users without restrictions, but after that, the number of people you can follow will depend on how many followers you have.

- **Protected tweets**: If a user has protected their tweets, they will have to approve you before you can follow them.

- **You have been blocked**: If a user blocks your account, you can no longer follow them.

Followers

If people cannot follow you or your follower count is lower than expected, check the following:

- **Protected tweets**: If you have protected tweets on, you have to approve any new followers.

- **Unfollowed**: A user may have unfollowed you, deactivated their account or had their account suspended.

- **Blocked**: You may have inadvertently blocked a user. Check in their profile and unblock them using the drop-down menu.

MOBILE ISSUES

Twitter is incredibly mobile phone-friendly, but some users do come across a few issues:

Apps

Most problems caused by apps, such as being unable to log in, are often due to the phone's cache memory, so try clearing it to resolve any issues (see your phone's user guide if you do not know how). If this fails to resolve the problem, remove your account from the app and then re-add it.

SMS

If you no longer want to receive SMS notifications or are having trouble with SMS tweets, just text 'STOP' to your Twitter short code (see page 172). However, text 'START' to reinitiate notifications.

TOP TWITTER CLIENTS

Throughout this book, we have mentioned a few third-party apps, clients and web services. However, many more third-party services are available that can help you maximize your Twitter experience. Here are some of the most popular (please note, due to Twitter regularly changing its access to third-party apps, some of the following services may no longer be available since this list was compiled). As prices are subject to change, we have indicated only if a client is free or paid for; see individual app or client for further details.

TEN TOP TWITTER CLIENTS

TweetDeck
(https://tweetdeck.twitter.com/)
Windows/Mac OSX • Free
Twitter's official client provides features not available using the web-based services, such as multiple account management, custom timelines and tweet tracking.

HootSuite
(https://hootsuite.com)
Windows/Mac OSX • Free/Paid Pro version
HootSuite lets you manage multiple Twitter accounts, track and schedule tweets, and provides features for other social media platforms.

MetroTwit
(http://www.metrotwit.com/)
Windows • Free/Paid version
MetroTwit is packed full of features including desktop notifications, built-in URL shortening, tweet filtering and list management.

Sobees
(http://www.sobees.com)
Windows • Free
A Twitter client that boasts plenty of features, but also lets you incorporate Facebook and LinkedIn with your Twitter accounts.

Tweetium
(http://tweetiumapp.com)
Windows 8 • Paid
Tweetium includes some unique features such as username auto-complete, pinned lists, live tile notifications, and integration with Windows Share.

Twitterrific
(http://twitterrific.com/mac)
Mac OSX • Paid
Offers multiple account management, intuitive synchronization, saved searches and lists, as well as foreign tweet translation.

Echofon
(http://www.echofon.com/twitter/mac)
Mac OSX • Free/Paid ad-free version
Along with the multiple account management and scheduled tweeting, Echofon lets you drag and drop media files into tweets.

Kiwi
(http://kiwi-app.net)
Mac OSX • Paid
A simple-to-use client that boasts a large number of design themes as well as some useful features, such as media previews.

Janetter
(http://janetter.net)
Windows/Mac OSX • Free
Plenty of visual customization options, as well as support for multiple accounts, image previews and pop-up notifications.

Triberr
(http://triberr.com)
Windows/Mac OSX • Free
While not strictly a Twitter client but a blogging tool, Triberr's integration with Twitter makes it a must for bloggers wanting to share posts with the Twitterverse.

TEN MOBILE TWITTER APPS

Twitter Mobile
iOS/Android/Nokia/Windows/Blackberry • Free

The official Twitter app is available for both Android and iPhone and simplifies the web-based service to make it more mobile friendly.

Plume
Android • Free

A fast Android app that lets you manage multiple accounts and make lots of customizations to your Twitter profile.

Tweetbot
iOS • Paid

The iPhone's most popular Twitter app, Tweetbot allows you to build multiple timelines, and customize and simplify your navigation.

Tweetr
iOS • Paid

An easy to use iPhone app for switching between multiple accounts, scheduling tweets and integrating multimedia.

Echofon (mobile version)
iOS/Android • Free/Paid Pro version

A fast and simple-to-use Twitter app that offers push notifications, inline photo previews and has an intuitive interface for ease of use.

Ubersocial
Android/iOS • Free

Ubersocial's moveable menu bar lets you show/hide various functions, and includes one-tap composing for speedy tweeting and multiple account management.

Carbon
Android • Free

This Android app provides extensive features including in-app YouTube and Vine video playback, full web page support from links and a tilt timeline.

HootSuite (mobile version)
Android/iOS • Free

Does basically everything the desktop version does, letting you manage all your social media platforms on your phone.

Twitterrific
iOS • Paid

Features include design colour customization, hashtag filtering for your timeline, push notifications and voiceover support.

PocketTwit
Windows • Free

One of only a few Windows Mobile-only Twitter apps, but PocketTwit has everything you need, including multiple account management.

TEN TWITTER WEB SERVICES

Paper.li (http://paper.li)
Lets you create your own newspaper by automatically finding, publishing and promoting articles based on who you follow.

wefollow (http://wefollow.com/)
A simple Twitter directory to which you can add your name, providing a great way to discover new users you might share common interests with.

Twellow (http://www.twellow.com)
Branded as the Yellow Pages for Twitter, Twellow lets you add yourself to its directory based on your industry or topics of interest.

Klout (http://klout.com)
Measures your influence on Twitter and other social networks by giving you a score out of 100, depending on the number of retweets, follows, mentions and other interactions you receive.

Twitter Counter
(http://twittercounter.com)
Lets you track your follower-to-following ratio, and provides graphs and statistical information, as well as forecasts of the number of followers you can expect to receive in the future.

Justunfollow
(http://www.justunfollow.com)
Lets you keep tabs on who has unfollowed you, new followers, fans and the least active people you follow.

PollDaddy
(http://twitter.polldaddy.com)
Lets you create simple polls that you can embed in your tweets to add spice to your interactions.

Friend or Follow
(http://friendorfollow.com)
Another follow-and -follower management website that lets you track who you have followed who has not followed back.

Contax (http://contax.io)
Tracks your followers and friends on Twitter and other social networks to keep you abreast of who other people are following and who is worth following back.

TwitBlock (http://twitblock.org)
Lets you discover if any of your followers are spamming or are bots, as well as allowing you to block tweets from people without actually unfollowing them.

INDEX